S

m Delaney is a writer and broadcaster whose journalism
ıas appeared in the *Guardian* and the *Sunday Telegraph*.
Ie is now the editor of *Heat* magazine and has written
nd presented documentaries for the BBC and Channel
'our. This is his second book. He lives in London with
his wife and daughter.

Also by Sam Delaney

Get Smashed! The Story of the Men Who Made the Adverts that Changed Our Lives

NIGHT OF THE LIVING DAD

CONFESSIONS OF A SHABBY FATHER

SAM DELANEY

JOHN MURRAY

First published in Great Britain in 2009 by John Murray (Publishers)
An Hachette UK Company

First published in paperback in 2010

1

This is a true story although some names and identifying characteristics have been changed to protect people's privacy.

A CIP catalogue record for this title is available from the British Library

ISBN 978-1-84854-094-1

Typeset in Bembo by Servis Filmsetting Ltd, Stockport, Cheshire

Printed and bound by Clays Ltd, St Ives plc

John Murray policy is to use papers that are natural, renewable and recyclable products and made from wood grown in sustainable forests. The logging and manufacturing processes are expected to conform to the environmental regulations of the country of origin.

John Murray (Publishers)
338 Euston Road
London NW1 3BH

www.johnmurray.co.uk

For Coco

CONTENTS

I
TRAVELCARD

We are in the bathroom. It's late. I've just cleaned my teeth and gobbed the minty residue down the plughole. I feel sexy. My wife is standing beside me, rubbing some sort of gunk into her face, when I turn to her and say, 'I think we should start trying for a baby right now.'

She stops rubbing and adopts this 'I don't know what to say, this is all happening so fast' look. At least, I think that's what it is. She may even be going a bit teary. Or maybe that's just some exfoliating grit in her eyes.

Then she says, 'OK, great. I'll come off the pill. We should be ready to get going in a couple of weeks.'

'A couple of weeks!' I think. 'When I said right now, I meant right now!' But apparently it takes a fortnight for the pill to wear off. Stupid pill.

I begin to realise that there's been a bit of a misunderstanding. When I said, 'I think we should start trying for a baby right now,' she must have thought I meant 'I think we should ACTUALLY start trying for an ACTUAL baby right now'. Whereas what I really meant was 'Shall we have sex right now? Please?'

But there you go. Now we're going to start trying for a baby. All because I couldn't think of a more elegant sexual advance on a run-of-the-mill Wednesday evening. Oh well. It was bound to happen sooner or later, I suppose. We both want kids. We just hadn't discussed exactly when. We've been in love for, like, ever. And one of the lesser-mentioned characteristics of a loving relationship is the lack of discussions you have about stuff. Not because, as cynics would have you believe, you're bored and have absolutely nothing left to say to each other. It's just that you know each other far too well to bother with much in the way of conversation. You share thoughts instinctively. She's hungry when I'm hungry. I'm happy when she's happy. Sometimes, although only occasionally, we simultaneously find ourselves inexplicably wanting to listen to Cyndi Lauper records. That's love. It gives us a mental affinity that makes talking largely unnecessary. Like that magical telepathy shared by Tony Cottee and Frank McAvennie in West Ham's legendary 1985/6 season. Each of us just knows what the other is thinking.

I've known my wife since school. I had a crush on her when I was about fifteen and finally managed to get together with her when I was twenty. We've been through all of life's key moments in each other's company. We collected our exam results together. We went to each other's grandma's funerals. We watched 9/11 unfold on the box, clutching each other's hands. We did the same when Take That broke up. Once we went on a daytrip to Alcatraz and took the audiotape guided tour together. Those kind of shared experiences fuse your very spirits together. She is pretty much better company than any of my friends. She's funny and gorgeous and smart. She devours a couple of books a week. Not only that, but she's thoughtful enough to buy me stuff to read while she's ploughing through her latest work of literary genius. The other day she got me a book of prison slang. Best thing I've ever read. See what I mean? She's my soulmate.

We've had a few ups and downs, I suppose. Once, about twelve years ago, I thought it'd be funny to hide from her when we were alone in my mum's house. It was just supposed to be a joke. I crouched behind a cabinet in the front bedroom. She started calling out for me, but I just stayed there giggling to myself. She hated it; it freaked her out, and she said she'd dump me if it ever happened again. What else? Oh yeah, once she had a dream about me and an imaginary foxy redhead ganging up on her at a party and ending up snogging in the corner. She was furious when she woke up. 'Don't worry baby, I won't leave you for the imaginary foxy redhead,' I said. And I wouldn't. But I must admit I still fantasise about that fictitious crimson beauty from time to time. Hey, it's not my fault. She was the one who invented her.

I can't really remember her ever upsetting me much. There was the time in New York on new year's eve in 1998. She got so drunk that I found her asleep with her head on the shoulder of a Chinese businessman in the queue for the bogs. He looked petrified. Later that night she puked on the bed in my cousin's apartment. I was briefly pissed off at her for about six hours the next day, but since then I can't recall many complaints.

I can't imagine what she sees in me. I'm not rich. My looks are adequate at best. I am intellectually inferior to her on a grand scale, and my line of chatter can, by common consent, be really, really irritating. Mind you, I have always been quite lucky when it comes to finding parking spaces. So I suppose I've got that going for me.

Anyway, the point is, I think we're probably ready to have a kid together. We both love kids. There's always been a tacit understanding that we would have them one day. We've never discussed exactly when – it just always seemed to be something we would do in 'the future'. Well, I suppose the future is now. Yes, I know that's a slogan from a mobile phone advertising campaign. But what better way is there to navigate yourself through life's biggest and most confusing decisions than via reference to advertising slogans? This is the game of life we're playing, and advertisers are pretty much the only ones who are bothering to show us the way it should be played.

I reckon we're ready to do this. We're not destitute. We've got our own place. Neither of us is mad or drunk or racist. We probably pass for reasonable parenting material. People have been asking us for some time when we might start a family. Nosey bastards.

'I don't know when we'll get round to all that,' I tell them sheepishly.

'Why not?' they persist.

'FUCK OFF! That's why not!' I reply.

I mean, what's it got to do with them? And what makes them assume that we're going to let social convention dictate our every life choice? Do we really seem so traditional and dull? My wife's a vegetarian, for fuck's sake. I moisturise. We're hardly Terry and June.

While I'm thinking over all of this crap, my wife seems to have warmed to the theme of me impregnating her. She is talking about maternity leave cover. There's no turning back now.

'We'll need a bigger car, I'd imagine,' I hear her say.

'Yep, you're not wrong,' I interrupt, clambering into the bedroom wearing a towel. 'Right then, better get started. These babies don't make themselves you know.'

And, do you know, I am having it off not five minutes later? If only I'd used a line as pithy and romantic as that in the first place.

After the sex she isn't pregnant. A couple of days later we do it again, and she still isn't pregnant. A whole month goes by, and still no sign of a baby. Frankly I am disgusted. What sort of a bloke am I? The sort of bloke who needs his testicles examined in case of deficiencies, that's what sort.

The last time I went to the doctors to have my nuts examined, I fainted, had a seizure and pissed myself. I'd thought I could feel a lump. So I went down the health centre and told them they'd better have a look. The doctors were busy, so the nurse had to do it in a side-room. I know, I know: it all sounds like an ill-thought-out plotline to a porno doesn't it? But it really happened. She told me it'd be easier if I stayed standing and dropped my pants. I did so, and she started tickling my scrotum. Sounds nice, right? Only it wasn't – it made me feel nauseous and dizzy. And the next thing I knew I was coming round on the floor in a puddle of my own piss with a couple of doctors fussing about me.

'Are you epileptic?' one of them was asking over and over again.

'What does it look like to you?' I said. From past experience it was immediately clear that I'd spent the last couple of minutes spazzing about on the floor, spraying wee all over the place and gurning like the big eppy bastard I am.

'Yes, it looks like you're epileptic,' said the doctor. Then he just walked out of the room.

'Are you on medication?' asked the nurse.

'No,' I mumbled, pulling my saturated trousers back on. 'It's not bad enough for medication. I only tend to have fits when I'm, erm, you know, in a state of high anxiety.'

An awkward silence befell the room. I decided to go. She showed no signs of stopping me.

'What about my balls?' I said as an afterthought, just as I was leaving.

'Oh yes, them,' she said. 'I definitely felt something strange. You should probably get them looked at by a doctor.'

I didn't say anything. But I did give her a look that I hoped said something along the lines of 'No shit, Florence Fucking Nightingale!'

Anyway, I didn't have ball cancer, if that's what you're waiting for. It was just a harmless testicular cyst, which is actually still there today and . . . hey, hang on a minute! What the hell has this got to do with anything? You don't need to know about my harmless testicular cyst.

Suffice to say, going back for another examination on my nuts isn't something I'm likely to enter into lightly. In fact, it isn't something I enter into at all. I decide instead to continue worrying about my virility in tortured silence. More months go by. Every time my wife has her period, she cries a bit. Increasingly, I find myself standing naked in front of the bathroom mirror angrily chastising my own genitals.

'You useless, lazy bastards!' I shout at them as they hang there all apologetically like a dog that's been caught pissing on the duvet. 'All you've ever done is cause me trouble! You've been like an albatross around my neck from Day 1! And now this! This really is the last straw. I've half a mind to cut the pair of you off!' But they refuse to respond to bullying tactics.

I fell into this situation almost by accident, and now it's dominating my every thought. Communication with my wife has all but disintegrated beyond blunt, emotionless texts and e-mails that say things like 'prgnt yet?' She responds with things like 'period strtd. ☹' Trying for a baby truly sucks the poetry from a relationship.

I'm probably approaching the whole thing in the wrong way. You're supposed to relax, chill out, think positive thoughts and have it off with your wife just like it was any other romantic night. Forget about the whole insemination process. Light some candles, put on some Luther Vandross, do it all slow and gentle. But come on: how likely is that? Once you know the sex is for something other than mere, frivolous pleasure, you're stuffed. You approach the whole thing like a robot. I can't get going without images from one of those spooky sex education films they showed you at school flashing through my brain. The sperm swimming its way towards the egg and all that. For some reason I start to hear David Attenborough commentating on my sexual performance while I'm trying to go at it. It's not nice. I try to refocus my brain, but all that pops in is Bruce Forsyth prancing about in flares singing 'Life is the name of the game'.

Another week goes by. Still no baby. Why am I so

impatient? Spoiled by rampant consumerism probably. I've grown used to having my every material wish fulfilled at the click of a mouse. iPods, Japanese carving knives, Princess Di memorial plates: all I have to do is type in my AmEx number and they're on my doorstep within a couple of days.

But you can't get a baby from Amazon.co.uk. Madonna's probably tried it, mind you. But me, I'd rather grow one organically in my wife's tummy if I can.

It is Friday night, and I am getting drunk in a pub. My wife texts: 'When r u cming home?' It's rather more verbose and polite than our recent communiqués. 'Something fishy's going on here,' I think to myself. 'Gtng drnk,' I text back. 'Dn't get 2 drunk ;),' she responds. Hang on a minute! Semi-colon followed by closed bracket equals saucy emoticon! Of course: it's sex night! Like I say, the poetry has temporarily been removed from our relationship. We're no more than colleagues working on an important joint project.

A couple of weeks ago we paid a doctor with a double-barrelled name 250 quid to help get us pregnant. After a bit of jiggery-pokery he managed to pinpoint the exact days my wife would be fertile. He even wrote them down for us on a bit of embossed notepaper (which I thought represented fantastic value for money). Turns out, there's only two days a month she's actually ovulating. Having it off at any other time is basically a waste of time. But tonight is one of the special nights.

'How could you forget?' she asks when I get home.

'I lost the list of dates!' I tell her.

'I've got the list of dates!' she exclaims, waving the embossed notepaper at me.

'But I copied them out on to a Travelcard and put it in my jeans pocket but then I put the jeans through the wash, and now the Travelcard's gone all crumbly and illegible!' I niftily explain.

That's the kind of chat that passes for foreplay these days.

Next, we settle down for some of the most mechanical, half-cut but technically efficient sex we've ever had. As I'm doing it, I mentally recount all the beer and wine and crisps I've consumed that evening. 'Probably best we don't conceive tonight,' I think to myself.

We conceive that night.

2

COKE

'Can you ever forgive me for all those terrible things I said?'

I am standing in front of the mirror, stark naked, cupping my genitals in my right hand.

'I was confused. I was angry. I didn't mean it. How could I have not trusted you?'

My testicles just sit there as silent and inscrutable as ever. But somewhere amidst those gruesome folds of skin I think I can detect the smallest twinkle of pride. Perhaps even a little smugness. I don't mind. Let them have their moment – they've earned it. They've come through for me big-style this time.

'You and I have done this, old friends!' I beam at them. 'You and I have created a human life! We've had some adventures together in the past – but this? This must be our crowning glory!'

How do you feel when you find out you've impregnated your wife? Proud? Astonished? Warm and fuzzy? Terrified? No, you feel victorious. You clench your fist, punch the air, adopt an aggressive snarl and shout out loud, 'Get in there you bastard!' like you've just scored the winner at Wembley. At least, that's what I did. The tiny

Indian nurse who'd just given us the good news didn't know where to look.

The whole thing had developed into a sort of game in my head. For months I had become obsessed with hitting my wife's ovaries in the right place at the right time. During sex I would sometimes shut my eyes and picture that scene from the end of *Star Wars* where Luke fires his successful shot at the Death Star's vulnerable exhaust port, blowing it to smithereens. I can honestly say that when that softly spoken nurse gave us the results, I couldn't have been happier even if I really had just destroyed an evil intergalactic space station. But after a few days of rampant triumphalism, it was time to take stock.

After this one last rousing address to my testicles in the bathroom mirror I breathe deeply and ask myself, 'Are you ready to be a dad?' I dwell on my reflection for a while longer and conclude that I don't really look like one. Dads should be bigger. And hairier. And altogether more man-like. I'm still kinda skinny and awkward – like an adolescent who'd probably get picked last for a five-a-side. Plus, I have this perennially stupid look on my face that suggests I've just stuck a flaming dog turd on someone's front step, knocked on their door and run away. Dads shouldn't look mildly amused. They should look authoritative and grumpy.

'Nope, you definitely don't look the part,' I say to myself in the mirror. 'At best, you look like a warm but slightly retarded uncle – which is basically what you are. Still, you've got nine months to work on your look. The question is: can you *act* the part?'

*

It's about a month later. I'm in a beer garden in Norfolk. We're on holiday. My eldest brother is sitting beside me playing about with his phone. His daughter Daisy is there too. She's eight and has read all the Harry Potter books, like, four times. She reckons this qualifies her to verbally outwit me. She reckons right.

I've just ordered a Diet Coke. It's part of my training for fatherhood.

'A *Coke*?! Didn't you say Coke was bad for us?' Daisy says.

'Yeah, I did. But this is Diet Coke. It's different.'

She looks incredulous.

'Diet Coke, Coke, surely they're all the same?'

'No. It's the sugar in Coke that's bad. This is sugar-free – see?' I point at the words on the side of the can.

She examines them sceptically then looks at her dad and asks him, 'Does that mean I can have Diet Coke?'

'Erm, no,' he says, looking up from his mobile phone for a moment.

'Why not?' she asks.

'Um . . . well.' He glances at me worriedly. '*Don't get involved, go back to your precious phone*,' I snarl at him with my eyes. 'The thing is, Diet Coke has other things in it that are bad for you. Sweeteners and caffeine . . . and . . . that.'

Why did he have to go and tell her that? She's a Rottweiler, this girl. Give her a glimmer of an argument, and she'll clamp hold of it and not let go until she's tasted blood.

'Cock!' I shout at my brother almost involuntarily.

'Pardon? What did you say?' says Daisy.

'Coke!' I say. 'I said "Coke".'

'I thought you said "cock",' she persists.

'No, merely "Coke",' I mumble absent-mindedly, pretending to have seen an interesting bird hovering somewhere overhead. But she won't be distracted. It's like having Jeremy Paxman for a niece.

'What about it?' she demands.

'What about what?' I say. I have no idea where I'm going with this.

'Coke! What about Coke?!'

I feel like I'm being interrogated. Any minute now she's going to grab me by the hair and start slamming my face into the table.

'Coke . . . is . . . it!' I say, meaninglessly. 'It's The Real Thing! Always Coca-Cola!' For some reason I deliver the last line in a tuneless little sing-song.

'Hmmmm,' she says, dismissively. 'It's strange that you took so much time the other day telling me how drinking Coke was like drinking . . . what was it again?'

'Petrol,' I mutter, hanging my head in lament.

'Yes, like drinking petrol. So why are you drinking Diet Coke? Are you on a diet?'

'NO!' I bark, noticing my voice cracking slightly.

'My dad says Diet Coke is even worse than the normal stuff. You're drinking something that's WORSE than petrol.'

Clever little shit. You'll have something worse than petrol all over your head in a minute, I think to myself.

'Now, now – I didn't say it was worse,' my brother interrupts, rightly trying to sort out the mess he created. 'I just said it was probably as bad.'

She scowls at him. He shuts his mouth and goes back to his phone. Over the past eight years I've seen her systematically break his will and erode his spirit. Now he's not so much a dad as an obedient automaton, trained to do her bidding.

'Well?' she says, turning her death-glare back on me.

'Well what? What do you want?' I ask.

'Are you going to say sorry?'

'Sorry?'

'Yes, sorry. Sorry for telling lies. And for saying one thing and doing another.'

She is deadly serious about this. My mouth goes dry. I look around for help, hoping someone may intervene. My brother glances up and gives me this pleading look as if to say, 'Just give her what she wants. It's easier that way.'

No. Screw that. I won't be bullied by an eight-year-old. So what if she's read a load of books about some gaylord little wizard? I've got a degree and a driving licence. I'm a grown-up. I'm VAT-registered, for fuck's sake.

I straighten my back and broaden my chest.

'Look, I'm only trying to give you some guidance OK?' I bark. She grins. My brother gawps and looks like he's about to cross his chest and jump under a table.

'I'm your uncle and I'm trying to give you the benefit of my experience. That's what uncles do!' I'm getting louder. 'Yes, I drink Diet Coke! There, I've said it. Know what? I sometimes drink normal Coke too. I'm a *bad* man, aren't I? But it's too late for me now. See?'

I pull my lips open to reveal the semi-derelict condition of my teeth and gums.

'That's what drinking Coke does to you. Do you want

to grow up with teeth like mine? I doubt it. That's why I've tried to warn you. But frankly, if you just see my advice as a chance to point-score . . . if you just want to throw it back in my face . . . then I don't care if you drink Coke. I'll buy you a can right now if you want!' I'm actually reaching into my pocket for the money. 'And why don't you buy yourself a packet of fags while you're at it? They give you cancer by the way – but you probably know best, right?!'

I pause for breath. She looks thoughtful.

'How much are fags?' she asks.

'I dunno. About a fiver?' I say.

'Can I just have the cash?' she beams.

I've gone red in the face now. 'No, you cannot!' I say.

'Why not?' she asks, remaining irritatingly calm in the face of my increasing hysteria.

'Because,' I say, moving in closer and lowering my voice to a menacing whisper, 'you are a rude and selfish little girl.'

Her eyes well up a bit. I drain my Diet Coke, slam the glass on the table and stride off to the bogs. I feel like Clint Eastwood. To everyone else in the pub I'm just the six-foot-two bloke who shouts at cute little girls with pigtails until they cry.

'In retrospect, I probably could have handled that better,' I say to my brother later that evening. We are slumped in front of an open fire with large glasses of brandy balanced on our chests. He stares blearily into the flames and contemplates the matter for a moment. 'Possibly,' he muses. 'When it comes to dealing with kids, it's like what the police tell you when you have to go to prison.'

'What's that then?'

'Don't make eye contact, and don't enter into any sort of conversation.'

I'm not exactly sure what he means by this, but I think I catch his general drift. Don't fuck with Daisy.

I have three older brothers. All of them have children who are more confident, more articulate and miles better-educated than them. Even the ones who are still at nursery have already attained more academic qualifications than all of the grown-ups in my family put together. They go to good schools where they're sitting French vocab tests at the same age that the rest of us were still taking lessons in how to shit into a potty. Then there's the high-falutin attitudes they pick up in those places. Socio-economic advancement may seem like a good idea at first, until your kids come home from school and start sneering at you for spreading Flora on your bread roll instead of dipping it in chilli-infused olive oil.

My brothers and I grew up in an environment where there wasn't a particularly strong emphasis on the completion of homework – by our teachers or our parents. That's not true – I think my dad probably thought it was very important we did our homework. But seeing as he was living with his new girlfriend on the other side of town, he didn't have much of an opportunity to monitor the situation. My brothers probably completed about half a dozen pieces of homework between them over the years. And at least one of those would have been a picture of a teacher with a giant penis growing out of his ear, scrawled in crayon on the back of one of our mum's final demand statements. Creative but never likely to get you fast-tracked into the sixth form's Oxbridge entrance classes. That's if our schools had had a sixth form or any Oxbridge entrance classes, which they didn't. Mind you, mine did have two Commodore computers and a well-stocked snack machine in the sports hall foyer, so I can't complain.

Once I had muddled through school and into a sixth form college, I started to buckle down a bit harder. I'd learned from my older brothers' mistakes; I didn't want my education to pass me by. But still my academic efforts were often undermined by their boisterous horseplay around the house.

'What the fuck are you doing?' they would burst into my bedroom and ask me, just as I felt I was getting to grips with the second act of *A Midsummer Night's Dream* or the meaning of photosynthesis.

'Homework,' I'd say.

'Homework?' they'd scowl, their noses running with snot (they would usually be inebriated on strong industrial solvents). 'Homework?' they would say again, this time doing a special 'gay voice' and performing a little fairy-like twirl. 'I'll give you some homework.' Then they would kick over the small bookshelf beside my bed and give me ninety seconds to re-shelve every item.

I know that makes them sound like wankers, but they're all right really. I can't blame all of my educational deficiencies on them; I was also hindered by my own laziness and naturally average intelligence. That and the fact that there never seemed to be enough pens in our house. No matter how many my mum nicked from the stationery cupboard at work, they would always disappear. We eventually realised the dog was eating them when she started to puke up dark blue ink. Eventually she died of pancreatic cancer. Coincidence? Unlikely.

Anyway, the point is, I may not be Professor Stephen Hawking but I'm not exactly Benny from *Crossroads* either. While I'm not catastrophically stupid, I'm just dumb enough to be intimidated by small children with precocious vocabularies and the courage of their convictions. I get drawn into arguments with them, allowing them to get me all cross and confused. They toy with my mind and my emotions like a cat toys with a badly injured mouse that it can't be bothered to actually kill. I am beginning to realise that this has less to do with cleverness and more to do with maturity. At thirty-two years old I am not yet mature enough to communicate effectively with small children, let alone command their respect. Sometimes my nieces and nephews find me funny. Occasionally they may find me interesting. But I'm not sure how much they actually respect me. The only way I've ever been able to get any of them to do anything (such as stop crying or give me back my car keys) is by paying them. Putting all of this together, I begin to realise that I lack any semblance of fatherly *gravitas*. Which is bad enough when you only have to cope with other people's children every couple of weeks. But what about when I've got one of my own knocking about the house full-time? This is something that's starting to worry me.

I look at my brother (who is now asleep with a large glass of brandy spilt all down his front) and think that he may not be such an obedient automaton after all. He's more like a clever, white-collar criminal who has learned to survive among the savage bullies on the inside. He knows when to keep his mouth shut. He knows how to keep his nose clean. He knows where he can buy a crudely fashioned shiv with which to protect himself should things get dicey in the showers.

'You're the sort of con a bloke can rely on,' I slur at him drunkenly, patting him on the shoulder.

'Hrrrumph! What!' he says, waking up all of a sudden.

'Oh, I just said you know how to . . . y'know . . . do your porridge with dignity.'

'Fucking right,' he slurs, then quickly falls asleep again.

I notice that I'm making more and more prison analogies in relation to fatherhood. This is another thing that's starting to worry me.

3
SNICKERS

There's a nurse rubbing a big electronic stick all over my wife's stomach. It's covered in gel. The room is dark and quiet. Altogether, it's the sexiest experience I've had in weeks.

'See that blinking little light?' she says, nodding at the monitor in the corner of the room.

'No,' I think. 'Yes!' I say.

'That's baby's heart,' she explains flatly.

I squint and hear myself saying something like 'Wow' or maybe 'Cor blimey'. It seems important that I pretend to be able to see what's going on. And be moved by it. All I can actually make out on the crappy little screen is a load of pointless, grainy shadows. It's like the sort of rubbish telly a student would hire from Radio Rentals. The sort that doesn't even have Teletext.

'And that long line on the left-hand side?'

'Uh-huh,' I say, pulling my special fascinated face.

'That's its spine.'

I stop smiling and turn away. I don't want to see its spine. I don't even want to think about what this baby looks like until it's warm and cuddly and giggling at the array of hilarious faces I am planning on pulling for it once it's out. Spines aren't warm or cuddly – they're all spiky and cold and rubbish. Now the nurse is talking about the outline of the skull and the half-formed fibula. She's making it sound like a stupid fossil or one of those tiny, translucent, featherless birds you used to find lying dead in the bushes when you were a kid. I feel like I'm going to puke. I squeeze my wife's hand just a notch too hard. It's a squeeze that tries to say 'I love you and I love looking at tiny human life forms in their early stages of development'.

My wife blinks worriedly at the screen. I think about how she must feel: she's the one with this grotesque bag of flesh and cartilage swimming around inside her stomach, or womb, or whatever you want to call it.

'And that black splodge there looks like an ocular cavity', deadpans the nurse.

I don't feel sexy any more.

Back outside in the waiting room I have to stand around while they book my wife in for another round of unedifying intrusions. The receptionist hands me a Polaroid version of the black shapes we've just been looking at on the screen.

'Something for your pinboard in the office,' she smiles.

I stare at the baffling image, trying hard to muster some sort of emotional response, but it's no good. It just looks like the sort of picture your mobile phone accidentally takes in your pocket when you've forgotten to activate the keypad lock. People put pictures of their children up at work to brighten up their day and make people think of them as balanced and warm. If I stuck this up, people might think I was a cynic or a murderer or some sort of goth.

As it happens I don't have an office or a pinboard. Still, the receptionist wasn't to know that. Or was she? The only other bloke in the waiting room has 'office' written all over him. He looks like he probably works in a big, oak-panelled office with leather-bound books on the shelves, a decanter of scotch in the cupboard and an electric pencil-sharpener on his desk. He is shaved and suited and reading a broadsheet paper. His shoes are shiny, his face is big and red and his expression is serious. I am scruffy and scoffing a Snickers bar I just bought from the snack machine. I worry that he looks more like dad material than I do. He's not the sort of idiot who'd eat a Snickers for his breakfast. I bet he had something fatherly before he came out. Kippers, I'd imagine.

I keep one jealous eye on him while flicking through the leaflet rack, hoping to find one about sexual diseases with pictures of gigantic knobbly tumours growing out of someone's helmet. Meanwhile, the other bloke is carefully analysing the business pages. At least, he's wearing an expression that suggests that's what he's doing – I can't actually see the pages. Maybe he's just got a copy of *Take a Break* concealed inside. I doubt it, though, not with shoes as smart as his.

I should mention that we are in Britain's poshest NHS hospital. It's in a salubrious district of London where people could not only afford to go private if they wanted to but probably also refurb Claridge's with medical equipment and staff it with specially shipped-in obstetricians and élite midwife teams from California if they really needed to. But they don't, because they've got this place offering a similar level of service on their local high street. We qualify for this privilege by living right on the edge of the same borough in a not-quite-so-salubrious district. We are the beneficiaries of a massive postcode injustice. I think about the stinking, falling-to-pieces infirmary down the road where my mum had to have eyes lasered a couple of years back. I feel mildly guilty. I am quickly distracted from my guilt by the smart man, who I notice is looking at his watch and sighing irritably. 'He's got the right idea,' I think to myself. 'That's what a dad would do. Look at his watch and sigh irritably. Not sit here grinning and eating chocolate.'

If I was in a crappier hospital there'd be fewer blokes like him and more blokes like me. Maybe some of the blokes would be even worse than me. There'd be drunk men, smelly men and men who smoked fags and blew the smoke into their pregnant wives' faces; men dressed in their pants, men who had wet themselves and men with racist tattoos. In short, men who would make me feel better about myself. Men who, by comparison, would make me look like the very model of a sober and serious-minded father. I'd probably feel just like that man in the suit does now: superior, expertly groomed and a bit irritable in a calm, authoritative sort of way. On the downside, my wife might catch the MRSA virus and end up having the baby delivered by a work-experience porter using a maths compass in the corridor.

On balance, we're probably marginally better off being here.

The man with the shiny shoes looks up as his wife shows

him the pointless Polaroid image of their barely formed offspring. He glances at it with unconcealed ambivalence and checks his watch again. 'Yeah, you tell her!' I think. 'There was me wasting my time pretending to look at the stupid picture when I could have been, I dunno, checking out how Procter and Gamble shares were doing on the Nasdaq or something. They probably hand the same bloody picture out to everyone anyway. I feel like such a fool. If only I had the confidence of the man with the shiny shoes.'

My wife comes back over from the reception desk.

'What are you singing?' she asks.

'Singing? I wasn't singing,' I say.

'Yes you were,' she insists. 'Under your breath. It sounded like the theme tune to *The Man with the Golden Gun*.'

Oh yeah, hang on, I think I was singing.

'"Shiny Shoes",' I say.

'What?'

'I was actually singing "The Man with the Shiny Shoes". I changed the words.'

She looks incredulous, then glances around the room. She sees The Man with the Shiny Shoes. Then she looks back at me.

'Have you invented a song about that man?' she asks.

'Keep it down,' I hiss, ushering her towards the exit.

Outside she asks me again. 'Well, have you?'

I tut, sigh, look at my watch a bit then say, 'Yes, OK, I have invented a song about that man.'

She looks disappointed.

'The Man with the Shiny Shoes was a dick,' she says.

'Oh . . . yeah . . . total dick,' I chuckle.

'Are you sure you didn't think he was a bit cool?' she says calmly. She knows about my roving eye. The way I look at other men. How I worry that I should be more like them and less like me. And how I sometimes express those worries via the medium of song.

'Yeah. The original words I was singing were . . . er . . . The Man with the Stupid Face,' I insist.

She ignores this.

'He ignored his wife the whole time he was there and didn't even bother looking at the crappy picture. I mean, come on! At least you pretended.'

I narrow my eyes. 'Who says I was pretending?'

'It's OK,' she says. 'I was pretending too. If you don't act interested, they might report you to social services in advance or something.'

We get in the lift and fall silent. I think about the possibility of social services receiving advance intelligence on us. I resolve to feign interest even harder next time we're here. Then I think about The Man with the Shiny Shoes. Maybe he wasn't so great. His wife didn't seem to like him much. I didn't once see him reassuringly squeeze her hand a notch too hard.

By the time we step out of the lift I'm feeling much better about myself. Just because I don't eat kippers for breakfast or understand the money markets doesn't mean I'll make a bad dad. This is 2007: get out of the '90s, you shiny-shoed dick! Everything you know is wrong! You're looking at the new face of modern parenting! Yes, that's right, it's covered in melted Snickers. Deal with it.

★

It's early evening, and I'm standing in a pub with my mate Dave. He is looking at me blankly while I brandish my black, pointless Polaroid in his face.

'That's baby's spine!' I beam, pointing at an arbitrary area of the photo. 'And that bit on the left is either its fibula or its ocular cavity, I'm not sure which.'

4

GREASE

I'm not really living the lifestyle of a responsible adult. This isn't how a dad goes about his business. I don't have a proper job. I'm a freelancer. When you tell people that, they think you're basically a layabout with pretensions. In fact, I work reasonably hard, but most of what I do is just namby-pamby nonsense. Writing stuff, talking jibber-jabber on the TV and radio: it's hardly the gritty and industrious vocation of an honest-to-goodness father figure. I don't come home from work with roughened hands and weather-battered features; I usually pull up in a black cab with a takeaway. And I don't have a pension or savings or anything like that either. I have not really been cultivating a safe and secure nest in which to raise this child.

Still, I've managed to wrestle my way out of that long post-student period of constant financial peril and into a strangely comfortable position where I can spend long afternoons in the gym or the pub and still manage to pay my mortgage every month and have a bit left over for new trainers and sweeties and that.

My flat is swish: the floors are made out of black rubber, and the kitchen is made out of imported Italian wood or something – I dunno, the people we bought it off had it installed. There is a widescreen plasma mounted on the wall and stupid pieces of 'art' hanging everywhere. There is an expensive sound system, an elaborate, unused coffee machine and a stylish, profoundly uncomfortable L-shaped sofa. Altogether, my flat is what can only be described as a bit poncey. It's like I'm some sort of cut-price Patrick Bateman out of *American Psycho*. There are no dead prostitutes in my fridge, but I sometimes wonder whether there might be if I weren't married to a level-headed woman who simply wouldn't stand for that sort of thing.

'Where are those Quorn sausages I bought, darling?'

'Behind the hooker's skull on the second shelf down. The one with the eyeballs removed.'

Also like Bateman, I have a tendency towards obsessive materialistic fetishism and conspicuous consumption. Nevertheless, I feel almost certain that I would never kill and refrigerate a sex worker.

This kind of lifestyle is quite nice, I suppose. It's better than I expected when I was a kid. The best-paid person in my house back then was my brother, who was working as an entry-level postman. I dreamed of living his life of 4 a.m. starts, cold days tramping the rainy streets, wearing a stinking nylon uniform. He told me such enchanting tales of stealing cash out of children's birthday cards and occasionally winning a tenner on the canteen fruity. The Royal Mail sorting office sounded like bloody Xanadu to me when I was ten. I could hardly dare to dream of one day living the same exotic lifestyle enjoyed by my brother. He had a motor bike and a girlfriend and a music system in his room. To my young eyes he was like Faceman out of *The A-Team* and Dex Dexter from *Dynasty* rolled into one.

But I didn't think I really had it in me to follow in his footsteps. He seemed to have a certain charm and mettle that I sensed were lacking from my flimsy soul. I figured I'd probably end up miserable, unemployed and alone in a shit-smeared bed-sit in Isleworth, crying my tits off in front of the snooker on a black-and-white telly.

So, all things considered, I can't complain about the way things have turned out. If I could travel back in time to 1985 and meet my younger self, he'd wet himself with excitement. Then my brother would probably come back from his night shift at the sorting office feeling grumpy, beat me up and steal my wallet. But it'd be worth it just to see the look on my podgy ten-year-old face.

Mind you, there's been a small concern nagging in the back of my mind for some time now that I am, in fact, entirely pointless. I'm making about as much valuable contribution to the progression of mankind as a member of the Pussycat Dolls. And not the fit lead singer one, either – one of the others who just stand around at the back.

God, I've wasted what little spare money I've earned. The iPod attachments, the games consoles, the taxis. All those luxury, overpriced biscuits. Maybe they are just a sorry excuse for something else. Something bigger. Something soft and cuddly that pukes on your new trainers when you're just about to head down the pub. I'm guessing that, once I have a baby and look into its cute little baby eyes, I will realise once and for all that all those shiny things were just worthless surrogates. There is also a slim chance I may get bored of the baby after a few months and realise that Pro Evolution Soccer wasn't such a waste of time after all. But by that time it'll be too late: I'll have eBayed my Xbox and used the proceeds to buy a papoose.

This flat is not child-friendly. There are breakable ornaments and dangerous spiky edges everywhere. Plus, I'm a weirdo neat freak who doesn't like it when my nephews and nieces come round in case they move a magazine.

The building is on a dirty street full of traffic and madmen. Some nights a drunk man stands out on the pavement shouting, 'You're all fucking wankers!' over and over again. He's probably angry at the world. But when I'm lying in the darkness unable to sleep, I worry that he might be angry at me personally. 'Who? Who are the fucking wankers?' I think to myself nervously. 'Am I one of them? Was I a fucking wanker to you in the past? I'm sure you've made a mistake. I've never been a fucking wanker to anyone! I swear on my life! I've been a twat. I've been an idiot. But a wanker? A *fucking* wanker? No, this must be some sort of terrible mix-up!' I think about going out on to the balcony and shouting, 'I'm not the fucking wanker you're looking for!' But instead I just lie there fretting for a few more hours until he goes away.

He's not the only problem. The other day some kids stole and vandalised my scooter. The same ones lobbed a water balloon at my mates on their way into the house. It was an ambush. I tried to have it out with them, but they pulled a knife. I told my wife I was going to go and get my Leatherman, but she stopped me by saying, 'What are you going to do? Have a knife fight like someone out of *West Side Story*?' She had a point. I can't knife-fight. Especially not rhythmically to music like they do in *West Side Story*.

In the hallways and stairs that lead to my flat there is a nasty, musty smell. The carpet is loose, and there are old fag-ends and chocolate bar wrappers lying around on the floor. I think there are about six or seven other flats inside. I can't be sure, because the faces I encounter on the stairs are always changing. When I see one of them, I stare at my feet and mutter. They do the same. All of us are trying to ignore the fact that we live cheek by jowl with strangers in a lonely building on a stinking polluted street where screaming and sirens punctuate our anxious nights. We're trying to tell ourselves that this urban nightmare is OK. That it's cool to be terrified and alienated. But I'm not sure I can suspend my disbelief any more; I fear my mask of sanity is beginning to slip.

From what I've seen of them, the neighbours are mostly bastards. They steal our mail and have parties. The bloke who lives upstairs is auditioning for an appearance on the ITV reality show *Grease is the Word*. He wants Simon Cowell to select him as the new Danny Zucco. He rehearses the song 'Sandy' continuously throughout the day. While I'm on the phone to the bank, all I can hear is him warbling on about being stranded at a drive-in.

'What was that?' says the woman in the Indian call centre.

'I said I wanted to extend my overdraft,' I reply.

'You mentioned something about a drive-in?'

'Forget the drive-in. Just give me the money.'

The same neighbour also enjoys singing 'Walking in Memphis', by Marc Cohn. 'That won't get you anywhere with Cowell,' I think smugly to myself. 'It's not even in *Grease*. Do your bloody research you shithead!' By late afternoon I start to think about going upstairs and cutting out his larynx with a tin-opener.

When I do eventually go upstairs and bang on his door, he falls silent and refuses to answer.

'I know you're in there,' I shout. I hear his breathing. I think about kicking the door down. 'I'm gonna kick your door down!' I shout.

But when push comes to shove, I don't think I've got it in me. I'm just hoping I can scare him into thinking I might. In the end I just write an indignant note and slip it under his door. That evening, while my wife and I are watching telly, the singing starts again. I jump up from the sofa and head upstairs for a confrontation. 'Don't be a dickhead about it,' my wife calls after me. But she knows I'm going to be a dickhead about it. I'm doing my special dickhead walk.

BANG! BANG! BANG! I am slamming my fist against Danny Zucco's front door. 'Open the door!' I shout. The singing stops again. 'I'm going to kick your door down,' I say. The neighbour from across the hall pokes his head out.

'Everything OK?' he asks.

'Fine,' I smile all politely. He disappears.

I hurry back to my flat and start rummaging around in the cupboard under the sink.

'What are you going to do?' asks my wife.

'I'll set fire to his flat,' I explain. She seems unconvinced.

'You can't burn his flat down. You'd never be able to isolate the flames! We'd all go down. You'd be burning your own home.'

She's probably right. And besides, all I can find is an old pan scourer and some Brasso. No one ever started a fire with that.

My wife e-mails Danny Zucco's landlord. The landlord threatens to evict him unless the singing stops. He moves out and things go back to normal. But it all leaves a nasty taste in the mouth. This doesn't feel like the sort of environment in which to raise a child.

Plus, the whole episode didn't reflect well on me personally. I didn't respond to the problem with what you might call fatherly aplomb. For starters, any father should possess a certain amount of calm, diplomacy and fire-starting know-how. I have proved deficient in all three.

It's this flat. It brings out the worst in me. It makes me look, feel and act like a twat. I want to live in a place where I will feel like a responsible adult capable of raising a child. I want there to be a shed where I potter about at weekends. I want there to be four different types of recycling bin for various forms of household waste, each with its own subsections. I want there to be tiles that need grouting. I want to know what 'grouting' means. I don't want to knife-fight with my neighbours; I want to have them over for a barbecue on a sunny bank holiday. Then, maybe if we've had enough to drink, we might choose to have a musical, *West Side Story*-style knife-fight. But just for fun, as consenting adults.

I'm lying awake in the middle of the night worrying about the twatty flat and the horrid area and the way it all makes me feel so stupid and incapable. It's dark outside. No one is shouting swear words. No one is singing 'Sandy'. All I can hear is the gentle whirr of the air-conditioning system. That's because I am on the twenty-eighth floor of a hotel casino in Las Vegas. We flew here on a whim two nights ago to celebrate a friend's birthday. Which somehow encapsulates everything that needs fixing about my stupid lifestyle before the baby arrives. I am full of jet lag, overpriced sushi and self-hatred. I look at my wife on the other side of the gigantic bed. She's all sleepy and pregnant. I think about the chaos and the grime and the knives and the singing and the water balloons back home. I grab her arm and shake it.

'We should move to the suburbs,' I tell her.

So we do.

5
SAINSBURY'S

I am standing outside our new house clutching a hammer and some pliers. They're just two elements of the whole new tool set I bought down at Homebase earlier this morning. That's the kind of guy I am these days: a tool set kind of a guy. I'm using them to remove the 'For Sale' sign from our front garden. My next-door neighbour knocked round earlier and complained that it was blocking out her sunlight.

'No problem, I'll get rid of that sign for you,' I told her perkily. 'I'll just go and grab my hammer and my pliers. From my toolbox. Which I keep in the cupboard under the stairs. Because that's the kind of guy I am!' She looked at me strangely and walked off.

I now own a house with a front garden that's got a tree in it. I am a tree owner, and there's nothing more grown up than that. I am wrestling with the 'For Sale' sign when my hand slips and I whack myself in the face with the pliers. 'FUCK OFF!' I shout loudly in pain. The neighbour comes to her front window and looks at me crossly. I shrug back at her boyishly in a manner that I hope suggests that I'm not the sort of guy who usually goes around shouting 'FUCK OFF!' all over the place.

You'll have also noticed that I'm now the sort of guy who refers to himself as a 'guy' instead of a 'man', 'bloke', 'geezer' or 'hobbledehoy'. A guy is more informal than a man, more sensible than a bloke, more approachable than a geezer and more reliable than a hobbledehoy. A guy is the sort of guy who has a toolbox in the cupboard under the stairs. The most unpredictable and crazy thing that happens in a guy's life is whacking himself in the face with some pliers during the course of a domestic chore.

I pick up the pliers and get back to work. As pedestrians walk past the house, I sense them looking at me and thinking to themselves, 'What a studious and adept young man. He'd doubtless make an excellent husband and father.'

They're a funny bunch round here. Where I used to live, there was such a mix. Rich kids with preposterous hairstyles and imported Japanese trainers shared the streets with dipso geriatrics wearing cats round their shoulders like scarves. There were American hedge fund managers, demented crack whores, yummy mummies, hoodies, kids armed with water balloons, kids armed with knives, Nobel Prize winners and a whole host of famous faces off the telly all living together in one square mile. All the rich ones pretended the poor ones weren't there. It's what they call a 'melting pot'. Round here there's more uniformity. For instance, I've noticed everyone – man, woman or child – wears sleeveless body warmers. Some are fleecy, some are waterproof, some are padded, but the one rule is that they can't have any sleeves. It's a universally observed dress code. It's like the parish council have passed a law on it or something. I shall have to start cutting off the sleeves from all my coats and jackets in case they fine me. It'll be another chance to use an item from my new tool set.

So far we haven't made any friends. We came close the other day, when we were approached by a crowd of posh-looking middle-aged people on the high street. They were handing out leaflets that publicised the opening of a new supermarket in the area and twittering loudly to anyone who'd listen. Usually I don't do stop-and-chats with strangers. If a gang of strangers had approached me in the street back where I used to live, I would have instinctively kicked the closest one to me in the nuts and then run for it screaming. But this was a new area, a new me and a new set of strangers, who, it has to be said, looked less likely to stab, rape or vomit on us. In the spirit of mature, convivial, suburban neighbourliness I smiled and approached them warmly, accepting their leaflet with a feigned expression of interest. My wife took one too and examined the headline.

'Ooh, they're opening a Sainsbury's!' she said excitably. 'Great!'

No. Not great apparently. Not great at all.

'Great?' frowned one of the leafleting throng. 'What's so great about it?'

My eyes quickly scanned the leaflet more closely, consuming enough invective to realise that this was no promotional campaign.

My wife had got the wrong end of the stick. In fact, she'd got so confused that it was debatable whether she had the stick at all. But there was no stopping her now.

'Well, most of the shops round here are crap, aren't they?' she grinned.

She was right, of course. We have moved to one of the last few districts of London that has more or less managed to resist the onward march of major retail chains. The high street is occupied by the sort of small local businesses that your modern ethical, eco-fascist is so fond of harping on about: there's gift shops and fishmongers, haberdasheries and florists, numerous independent wine merchants and an abundance of 'charming' little outlets purveying trinkets, curiosities, forget-me-nots and other useless crap. But if you want to buy a tin of baked beans, some J-cloths or a pound of spuds after 5.30 in the afternoon, then you're stuffed. The locals don't mind this because the twee inconvenience of it all makes them feel like they're living in some rose-tinted 1940s' fantasy – only with less rickets and rationing.

Still, this was neither the time nor the place to point any of this out to them. These people were zealots. A fire of hatred burned in their eyes. Hatred for convenience stores with their array of fresh, reasonably priced produce and late-night opening hours. Hatred for the modern way of life that these supermarkets embodied. And hatred for the likes of us with our fully sleeved outerwear and weak-minded susceptibility to Nectar points promotional schemes.

A hush befell them. They seemed to be forming an angry circle around us. They fixed us with glares that screamed, 'You evil, ignorant, supermarket-loving bastards.'

Then one of them let rip.

'It'll tear the heart and soul out of the neighbourhood!' she spluttered in a shrill falsetto.

'There'll be neon signs and trolleys! It will be an eyesore!' said another. Their voices formed an indecipherable cacophony. Everyone wanted to get involved. My wife and I took a step backwards, only to find our paths blocked by more angry campaigners keen to point out how stupid and selfish we were. Someone said something about the ozone layer. Another mentioned traffic density. I heard somebody use the phrase 'carbon-neutral zucchini'. None of this made any sense. I began to feel like we were in *The Wicker Man*. 'Oh God! Oh Jesus Christ!' I muttered like Edward Woodward being dragged to his death in that giant burning effigy. How will they kill us here? Tear off our arms with their bare hands then shove a load of organically grown, locally produced asparagus up our arses before dragging our corpses around the local streets tied to the back of a Toyota Prius as a warning to other nonbelievers? Suffice to say, we had yet to acclimatise fully to the local culture and customs.

People haven't stopped wanting to stop and chat, mind you. It's weird. On a sunny day like today they even come up to you in your own front garden for an unsolicited chinwag. For instance, right now, an elderly woman is asking me about the flowers growing in my garden.

'Is it evening primrose?' she is asking while pointing at something on my front wall that, to my eyes, looks like a colourful clump of bird shit.

Before I can respond, she's wandered up the garden path to take a closer look. If I didn't know better, I'd think this was some sort of stitch-up. I know she looks posh and old and respectable, but she could easily be a pikey casing the joint. She could have a couple of accomplices hiding round the corner ready to pounce out and cosh me over the head with a sock filled with gravel once she's distracted me with her phoney flower chat. They'll be moving in with their eighteen grubby-faced children before I know what's happening. Burning tyres in the back garden, keeping ferrets in the bath, trying to sell me back my own plasma. That's how these people operate. Well, they've picked on the wrong bloke this time. I'm not just any old suburban mug.

'Look, luv, I don't know what you're on about,' I interrupt. 'I'd like you to get off my property please.'

She looks a bit taken aback. The door opens, and my wife appears. She smiles warmly at the old woman. She's very naive sometimes, my wife. Wouldn't know a confidence trickster if one came up and kicked her in the arse.

Luckily I've already done enough to get rid of the old bag, who's scuttling back down the garden path looking well and truly rumbled. And upset. And a little bit scared too. 'Hmmm,' I think to myself, 'maybe there's a chance she wasn't a gypsy confidence trickster after all . . .'

'What did she want?' asks my wife.

'The plasmas and the laptops, I reckon,' I say casually, 'but she might just as easily have been after the copper wiring out of the walls. You can get a packet for that these days.'

My wife looks back at the woman's retreating figure. She is tiny and wrinkled and slightly harassed-looking.

'Blimey, good job you had your pliers then,' says my wife after a bit of contemplation. Then she walks back inside.

I suppose I'm just not quite ready to be a talking-to-strangers-kind-of-guy yet.

6

LOVE

I clamber through the front door wrapped in a thin membrane of sweat and pollution. I chuck my keys in the drawer, drop my bag on the floor and peruse the pile of mail sitting on the table. And then I see it, sitting ominously on top of all those unopened bank statements and final reminders. A brown A4 envelope with my name written on it. My name written on it in pink highlighter pen with bits of gold glitter glued all around the outside. A chill tingles up from my stomach and karate-chops me in the windpipe. I know what this is, and it's worse than anything from the bank or the gas company. This is a valentine's card. And not just any valentine's card either. It bears all the hallmarks of a home-made valentine's card. The sort that requires a visit to W.H. Smith to buy some coloured card and Pritt Stick. The sort of that requires real effort. The worst sort of valentine's card.

Especially when you've got in from work with nothing to offer your thoughtful wife in return. Mind you, why should I have? There has been a mutual understanding in this marriage for some time now that we just don't do valentines. Didn't we discuss this? Didn't we decide that all the tacky cards and overpriced roses and romantic set menus cheapened and homogenised our love? Or something like that anyway. I definitely remember us dressing up the decision with some sort of clever-sounding twaddle. We have both stuck faithfully to the deal ever since. It depends on both of us observing its unwritten principles. Instead of cramming a large dose of cheap, nasty, commercialised romance into a single day each February, we have resolved to sprinkle it evenly across the entire year. Just little touches here and there, like making unsolicited cups of tea or remembering to flush the toilet after you've used it. Those are the sorts of things that keep the magic alive. The point is, our valentine's amnesty has been functioning perfectly well for years. But it depended on neither of us blinking first – a bit like the Cold War. Well, now my wife has blinked, and we find ourselves in our own personal Bay of Pigs.

I cautiously open the envelope and slip the top few inches of the card out. Oh God. Oh, Jesus Christ. It's worse than I thought: a whole bloody cartoon strip. With pictures of chimpanzees cut out of magazines depicting my wife and me in a satirical rendition of our relationship history. I can't bring myself to read this. I feel guilty enough already, without finding out how hilarious and touching it might be.

Why has she done this? She must have known I'd have come home empty-handed. How am I supposed to respond at this late stage of the day? She may not have heard me come through the door. I could sneak back down the shops, I suppose. But what am I going to get round here that comes anywhere near the level of poignancy of a hand-crafted chimp-based photo story? A box of Miniature Heroes and a dusty old birthday card which I'd quickly have to modify with a biro on the way home? That's just insulting. I may as well face the music.

I shuffle sheepishly into the living-room wearing a flustered, unconvincing smile.

'This is hilarious!' I blurt as she gazes up at me from the sofa. Then, as if to really hammer the point home, I glance at it again and emit a theatrical and rather too loud 'Ha!' It comes out sounding a bit sarcastic.

'Happy Valentine's,' she beams. I sit beside her and give her a kiss on the lips

'Thanks! I haven't got you anything,' I say, spontaneously, deciding on a come-right-out-and-say-it-we're-all-adults-here-after-all sort of approach. She half-smiles. 'I thought we didn't do that sort of thing any more,' I continue, 'although this really is brilliant.'

She looks a bit upset. Her eyes glaze over, and she gives a weak smile, then says, 'Don't worry, I don't mind.'

None of this makes sense. My wife doesn't play these sorts of mind games. She doesn't go in for melodrama, sentimentality, emotional trickery or any of that other stuff that can muddy the waters of an otherwise sensible relationship. She tells it like it is, my wife. She gives it to you straight. And if you don't like it quite as straight as she gives it, then you'd better get out of the way because you're liable to end up losing an eye. It can be harsh, but at least you know where you stand. If anyone has a tendency to come over all emotional and unnecessary in this relationship, it's me. But right now, I have to say, my wife is acting like some sort of . . . girl.

'If I'd known the policy had changed, I'd have . . .' I begin, but it's too late. She is now crying. Properly crying, with tears dribbling unapologetically down her reddened cheeks and snot coming out of her nose and everything. I get that punch-in-the-stomach feeling I get whenever she cries.

Then she blubs, 'I'm just being silly.'

She's right, of course – she is being silly. But this is what life is like in our house these days. All the usual rules and procedures have been turned upside down. I am having to learn to expect the unexpected. It's this pregnancy business, see? My wife is unusually delicate and touchy. She is sensitive to the things I say. Over the years she has learned to be pretty resistant to the endless tirade of ridiculous, boorish and offensive balderdash that spills from my lips. She has developed an internal filter that helps drown most of it out. But lately the filter seems to have malfunctioned. Now she's listening to almost everything I say. That's all I need.

I hold her close. There's no point in trying to reason with her. Reason has taken a nine-month vacation and been replaced by hysteria. I just have to be 'understanding' and 'sympathetic'. I express these sentiments by stroking her hair and making her loads of tea. 'Wanna cup of tea?' I say in a special baby-like voice designed to denote sympathy. She accepts. I bring it to her with a garibaldi biscuit. She looks happy. I feel like I have fixed the situation.

Later on, while she is in bed with a book, I sit on the bog reading the card. It is as touching and hilarious as I had suspected. Damn. I feel guilty all over again. I am overwhelmed with an urge to do something, anything, to show her how much I love her. In the absence of anything material to give her, and it being too late to offer her another cup of tea, I resolve to try and have sex with her. I mean, what's more romantic than that?

'What are you doing?' she says. I am clambering around under the bedclothes in my own uncoordinated version of foreplay. I am clumsy and oafish. Even after all these years together she still can't really tell whether I'm trying it on, having a fit or looking around under the sheets for the remote control.

'I'm trying it on!' I grin, all proud of myself.

'Why?' she asks.

'Coz it's Valentine's?' I explain.

'But I'm in the middle of a chapter.'

I shrug and fall silent for a bit. She returns to her book. I keep staring at her. In my head my expression is seductive and predatory. I am burning through the pages of her weighty novel with sheer sexual electro-power. Soon the stupid book will fizzle and burn in her hands. And then her bra will burn also, but not so badly that it will harm her breasts in any way.

'What are you looking at me like that for?' she eventually asks.

'You know why,' I say, a bit like Roger Moore.

'Why are you talking in that stupid voice?' she enquires.

It's beginning to feel like *Twenty Questions*, so I decide to snatch the book from her, fling it across the room, switch off the lights and just make a lunge in the darkness. Sometimes a woman likes a man to be a man. To take control. To grab the night by the scruff of the neck, look it square in the eyes and tell it, 'Library time is over Daddio, it's time to get down and boogie with Dr Love.'

'What the fuck?' she exclaims.

'Oof,' I blurt as she accidentally skims my nuts with her foot. At least, I hope it was an accident.

'What's the problem?' I say. 'I'm just trying to be . . . what d'you call it? Affectionate.'

She flicks the light back on. 'I'm not up to it,' she says. 'I feel rubbish and tired. Sorry.' She turns on her side and shuts her eyes.

I decide to stay awake for a while, staring at the wall and feeling sorry for myself. I may be gormless and ungainly in the bedroom but she knew that when she married me. It's never bothered her before. Hanky-panky has been pretty much off the agenda for weeks now. She is always tired and tense. She says she feels unattractive. I've tried to tell her that, what with her breasts looking all pregnant and inflated, I actually find her more attractive than ever. It doesn't seem to help.

'Can I make you a cup of Horlicks?' I ask in the darkness.

'No,' she mumbles in a state of semi-consciousness.

'Ovaltine?' I venture.

'Shut the fuck up and go to sleep,' she says.

Times are tough, all right. The dynamics of this relationship have changed lately. She's usually so calm and in control. She's the rock we build our lives on; the voice of reason and the flag-waver for common sense. She's the one who stops me from doing stupid, irrational stuff like trying to burn people's flats down. If I tried to burn someone's flat down now, I don't know what would happen. She'd probably be too tired or tense to stop me. And then where would I be? Actually committing an act of stupid arson, that's where. It's a frightening thought.

It's not just that. My wife usually trims the hedges in our garden, sets up the direct debits at our bank and knows where all the heating controls for the house are. Let's be honest: she's the man of the house. Yes, it sometimes feels a bit humiliating. But not quite so humiliating that I have been bothered to learn how to do any of this stuff for myself.

Well, I'm having to learn now – and fast. She is becoming emotionally and physically incapable of performing her usual role as our home's father figure. It's time for me to step up to the plate.

The new house still needs a bit of work done on it. She has developed a fixation about every last detail being finished and perfect by the time the baby arrives. I'm not just talking about the flat-pack cot being assembled either. She wants the walls painted, the carpet fitted and those dangerous-looking wires hanging out of the wall in the baby's bedroom dealt with too.

'Don't worry, don't worry, I'll get it all sorted in time,' I tell her.

She looks at me sceptically. I can't even change a light bulb without lengthy reference to my *Reader's Digest DIY Manual*. Besides pulling down that For Sale sign, all I've used my tool set for so far is smashing up ice cubes to put in a glass of Dr Pepper.

Besides, even if I had the know-how, I wouldn't have the time. My days are busier than ever right now. With the birth drawing nearer, I feel under increased pressure to earn money: the child will doubtless be needing it to fritter away ungratefully on sweets and nappies and *Transformers* or what have you. And when I'm not actually out earning money, there is important time-wasting to be done. I figure once I'm a dad I won't have much opportunity to waste time any more: my life will become too hectic and filled with responsibility. That's why I'm trying to waste plenty of the stuff while I still can. I set aside a few hours each day to play Tetris on my laptop or just stare into space while idly wrapping my own hand in Sellotape. The other day I managed to sit through the whole of *Three Men and a Little Lady* on Sky Classics in the middle of the afternoon. I felt as if I owed it to myself.

There's no point trying to explain my frenetic time-wasting schedule to my wife, though. I just couldn't find the words to make it sound like a credible excuse for why the kitchen is still devoid of all essential appliances and we are keeping fresh food in a chilled picnic box next to the sink.

I make an executive decision to hire some men to do it all for me. My mate Simon is an expert painter and decorator. He says he can paint the entire inside of our house in three days. I hire him for two weeks, which he foolishly interprets as an act of generosity. What he doesn't realise is that I'll be needing him to fit light bulbs, install fridges, hang pictures and fiddle repeatedly with the heating controls during this period. Admittedly, these aren't the sorts of menial services he usually provides. But the bloke owns a van and a portable radio splattered with paint: if that doesn't mark him out as 'handy', I don't know what does.

I don't want to insult him by coming right out and asking him to do these odd jobs. I think it's more polite to subtly trick him into it. While he's on his lunch break, I ask him if he minds helping me hang this giant round mirror in the front room.

'Just stand there and tell me if it looks straight,' I say, holding it in position.

'Yeah, that looks about right,' says Simon, chomping on his sandwich.

I reach into my toolbox and fish out the hammer and a nail. I call it a nail – it's more of a tack really. It'd struggle to hold the weight of a set of door keys, let alone this 12-stone mirror I'm trying to put up. But it's all part of my ruse, see?

'What the fuck is that?' asks Simon in disbelief.

'It's a nail! What d'you think it is?' I say all casual, as I start to bash it cack-handedly into the wall.

Simon walks over and nabs it from me. 'You're not gonna hang anything on that. That's a girl's nail,' he says.

'Really?' I say. 'Well, it's the only sort of nail I've got. Maybe I should put a couple in?'

'No. You'll need more than just a nail. And you'll need more than that poxy craft hammer as well. I'll go and get my drill.'

And with that simple exchange I have Jedi mind-tricked Simon into performing what will be the first of many domestic chores over the next fortnight. I feel pretty clever, if a little hurt by what he said about my hammer. I make a mental note to go back to Homebase and buy something a bit chunkier as part of tomorrow's time-wasting itinerary.

Over the next few days, in between his painting obligations, Simon helps me wall-mount a TV in the bedroom, stick handles on all the cupboards in the kitchen, fit a new toilet seat and sort out those rogue electrical wires in the baby's room. He also helps me get in through the back door after I lock myself in the garden. Twice. I should feel like I've got him in the palm of my hand – but I don't. It hasn't taken him long to flip the dynamic back in his favour. Without asking, he has brought in an assistant called Ted, whom I have to pay extra for. The pair of them have started talking me into extra work that I never knew I needed.

'We can get hold of some cheap tiles to sort out that problem in the kitchen,' Simon tells me.

'What problem in the kitchen?' I ask.

'Damp,' says Ted. 'It's not too bad at the moment, but if you don't re-tile, it could be chaos in about a year.'

'How will re-tiling help?' I say.

'These are special damp-resistant tiles. They'll stop it penetrating any further.'

I stand there pretending to think about what they're saying. The truth is, whenever they go into the details of their work, my brain zones out and I start to visualise the Kleenex puppy in a pair of Ray-Bans dancing around to 'Money for Nothing' by Dire Straits. By the time I zone in again, they're explaining that they can get me the tiles at 50 per cent discount through a mate. I find myself agreeing to the deal.

'Great, well, are you gonna be in Fulham any time this afternoon?' Simon asks.

'No,' I say. I mean, why would I be in Fulham this afternoon? There's absolutely no precedent for me being anywhere near Fulham at any time of day.

'Only that's where the tiles need picking up from,' he continues, fixing me with his 'You're not going to make a big deal out of this, are you?' look.

Needless to say, I'm soon on my way to Fulham to pick up the tiles from a grumpy old codger on the North End Road. He's offish with me to begin with, until I tell him that Simon sent me. Then he perks right up.

'You his boy, are you?' asks the codger.

I'm not sure if he means this in a romantic or professional sense. Either way, I reply with an indignant 'No!' But he doesn't hear because his mobile has just started to ring. Only it's not actually ringing; it's bellowing out this 'comedic' announcement, which says, 'Can the man with the ten-inch penis please answer the phone immediately.' He answers the phone, shooting me a matey wink. I try my best to look unamused.

'Like my ringtone, did you?' he chuckles once he's finished his protracted chinwag.

'Not really,' I say, acting a bit sulky because he's treating me as if I were a teenager.

'Course you did!' he says. 'Now load them tiles in the motor and get back to the site before your boss gets the hump.'

'Site? Boss? Hump?' I think angrily to myself as I leave. 'This daft old loon has clearly got the wrong end of the stick about what the deal is between me and Simon.'

Only he hadn't. When I get back to the house, Simon tells me off for taking so long. 'But it was that mad old bastard with his ringtone!' I start to explain.

'Don't want to hear it,' says Simon. 'Me and Ted are gonna have to work late now.'

By 'late' he means past five o'clock.

I should put my foot down and remind everyone who's paying the wages around here. But I can't. Like I say, Simon is a mate. And anyway, I am in thrall to him and Ted: their magical handyman skills, their blokeish banter, their array of mystical tools and gizmos. Sure they patronise me, fleece me and mock me for what they see as my effeminate and flighty lifestyle. But they also let me use their sledgehammer to break up old tiles in the back garden and give me Jaffa Cakes. I'll miss them when they're gone. Which, as it happens, won't be any time soon. They claim to have discovered more damp and have, in response, smashed the whole room to pieces. We've got no sink or anything. We're having to do the dishes in the bath. I've no idea where the cooker has gone. I think they said something about putting it out back or throwing it in the canal or something. We are having to survive on whatever raw foods we can find in our bombsite of a home. The other night I ate twelve Cola Bottles covered in brick dust for dinner. It's got so bad that my wife's almost starting to wish I'd taken care of all the chores myself. Almost.

She wakes up feeling too sick and weary to go to work one morning. 'Take the day off, it's important you look after yourself,' I say. There's something exciting about her being around the house during the day. It feels like when the teachers go on strike when you're a kid and you get an unexpected day off school. You've suddenly got a licence to muck around while everyone else is out at work. It's anarchic. Of course, I really should be at work myself. Or wasting time. Or running errands for Simon and Ted. But

I tell myself that hanging out with my wife is more important: she needs my support.

We sit around watching telly and eating biscuits. We go out for lunch together. We basically act like a retired couple for the day. Over lunch we talk about possible names for the baby: I like Napoleon, Zeus or Jesus (pronounced 'Heyzus', like some sort of maverick South American centre forward) for a boy and Shee-ra or Princess for a girl. She remains non-committal about all of them. Ultimately, I don't suppose I'll get the final say on the matter. I guess I'll just wait and see what her decision is on the day of the birth.

One other development: she suddenly wants to have sex again. Like, all the time. It's weird – this happens in the final few months of the pregnancy apparently. Trouble is, her bump has now grown so large that the sheer mechanics of congress are too complicated for me to even attempt. I'm not the most dexterous fella at the best of times. I struggle to perform even the most rudimentary sexual manoeuvres. To attempt anything saucy with her now would just be dangerous – I could pull a hamstring, crack a vertebra or worse. Plus, the baby's on the move. It's kicking and dancing around in there like nobody's business. You can actually see its little hands trying to punch their way out of the womb while my wife lies on the bed. It's off-putting. I don't want to feel my unborn child moving while I'm trying to get busy with my missus. Let's be honest, it's noncey.

'I'm not up to it,' I tell my wife.

'What's up?' she asks.

I don't want to make mention of the size of the bump

or its tendency to move and jerk about. Those are sensitive subjects. So I just say, 'I feel, erm, you know, tired and tense and . . . unattractive.' Well, it worked for her.

She laughs a bit. Then does a bit of a cry. I hold her apologetically and contemplate the fact that this is the first time in my life I have ever been in a position to turn down sex. And it'll almost certainly be the last.

7

BOBA FETT

I've been awake for what feels like hours. I wonder why my eyes won't adjust to the darkness. It may be that I've lost track of whether they're open or shut. 'I wonder what it would be like to go blind,' I think, in a way that only someone who's been lying awake in bed for hours can possibly think. 'Shit, maybe I am going blind. I keep getting those headaches. Must go to the optometrist. Or optician. What's the difference? Nobody knows. They don't just check your vision; they examine your eyeballs for cancerous growths. Eye cancer. Imagine if I had that. Blood seeping out of your corneas like tears. Jesus, anything but that. That or throat cancer. Or brain cancer. Anything inside the head. Cancer of the goolies I could manage. OK God, here's the deal: if I have to have any form of cancer, I'll take goolies. I've already got my missus pregnant – they can lop the bastards off now for all I care. We'll adopt a second. From Africa maybe. They could do with a few more black faces in an area like this, it's like *Village of the Damned* round here. Either way, I'm calling the optometrist first thing in the morning. What time is it? 4.19 a.m. Already? Now I'll never get back to sleep. Shit! Why did I check the clock?'

My wife fidgets beside me, trying to negotiate her ripened bump into a comfortable position. Her irritable night-time sighs are the only sounds that punctuate the pitch-black suburban silence. There are no street lamps outside our house and no traffic either. It's spooky. For a brief moment I miss the man who used to call us all fucking wankers at night. At least he reminded me that I was alive. But I suppose peace and quiet was one of the reasons we came here. It's just proving more of an acquired taste than I imagined.

Engine noise is what I miss most. The rumble of freight vehicles. The violent whine of super-bikes racing in the dead of night. The hiss of brakes on a National Express coach. These are the sounds that soothed me to sleep throughout my childhood. Our house was perched on the side of the A4 in west London. My bedroom windows shuddered with the vibrations of lorries and buses as they trundled by each night. It was rhythmic and comforting – like sleeping on a train. Plus, all the pollution formed a sticky black residue on my bedroom windows, which helped dull the neon glare of the street lamps that shone outside.

We'd been living on the grim sprawling estate down the road until our dad did the off. Understandably, my mum went temporarily loony and the family doctor identified us a family at risk. At risk of what was unclear: but four young sons plus a half-mad mother living on an estate where the opportunities for trouble were plentiful was probably considered a recipe for disaster. So they moved us to the little house on the motorway. I guess they figured that the carbon monoxide in the atmosphere would be slightly less damaging to our health than the inexpensive heroin that was available back on the estate.

Mind you, the new place was hardly a sanctuary of peace and quiet. Anarchy reigned from the moment we moved in. I was about six, and my three brothers were in their mid-teens. They fought and swore and abused drugs. My mum was traumatised, abandoned and skint. She worked as a part-time secretary, finishing at half three every day so she could pick me up from school. Driven to desperation by household overheads, the financial demands of her adolescent sons and her own cavalier use of a Dorothy Perkins store card (which she used to indulge in a rather perverse, prototype form of retail therapy before the term had even been invented), she ended up going to loan sharks for assistance. Even my school uniform was financed by a local Irishman in a grubby suit with a thin, insincere smile and a competitive line in 75 per cent interest rates. Every Friday evening he'd knock round for the latest repayment, then outstay his welcome by sitting on the sofa and trying it on with Mum while I tried to concentrate on *Play Your Cards Right.*

A constant stream of unsuitable dossers passed through our house. Drunks, degenerates, thieves, scoundrels and thugs all used our home as a place to stay for a night or sometimes more. And those were just the ones Mum invited back.

She sympathised with lost souls and offered them sanctuary under our roof: the dipso Glaswegian milkman, the hunchback machinist from the signage company where she worked, the flighty junior from the typing pool who'd just split up with her husband. That particular dosser actually came downstairs one night dressed in a slinky négligé and tried it on with my brother, who must have been at least eight years her junior. That sort of thing never once happened to me when I reached seducible age, which is just another indication of the rampant injustice that prevailed in our household.

Late one night I answered the door to a middle-aged woman who looked like she'd just gone eight rounds with Lloyd Honeyghan. Beside her stood a small boy about two years younger than me, dressed in his jimmy-jams and crying. She turned out to be the lady who brought round the sandwiches at Mum's office. They were invited to stay for as long as they liked. Looking back, it was an admirable act of instinctive compassion by my mum. After all, this woman wasn't even a close mate – she'd just tipped up knowing that my mum was the sort of person you could turn to in those sorts of situations. But as Mum uttered her invitation, all I could do was look at that poor, traumatised lad – a boy who had obviously witnessed despicable scenes of domestic violence that no child should ever have to see – and think to myself, 'That little shithead needn't think he's kipping in my room.'

Yeah, his dad may have knocked his mum around a bit. Yeah, he'd had to flee his family home in the dead of night and move in with a bunch of strangers. All that might have gone some way to explaining WHY he was a little shithead but it didn't make him any less of one to my mind. Needless to say, he DID get to kip in my room, play with my toys, wear my clothes, nick stuff from my lunchbox and generally fuck with my shit for the three months they stayed with us. He'd pester me and attack me, verbally abuse me and continually switch the telly over when I was trying to watch *Saint and Greavsie*. I'd always been the little brother of the house. Suddenly I had one of my own and I didn't like it. If I complained, or moaned or punched him in the stomach, I'd be the one who was condemned.

'Poor little Jimmy, all he's been through! Why don't you give him a break?' my mum would ask.

'Jimmy's a wanker,' I told her.

She'd just tut, shake her head and give him the last packet of Golden Wonders from the bread bin to make him feel better. Even my brothers were on his side. They never made him do the bookshelf challenge once. They quickly worked out that taking his side in any conflict was a brilliant way of winding me up into an incandescent state of frustration.

'Jimmy, you took that pound coin from my piggy bank, didn't you?' I once shouted at him in the living room.

'Tell him to fuck off, Jimmy!' my brothers chuckled.

'Fuck off!' Jimmy grinned. Instinctively I lunged for him, only to be intercepted by my brothers, who encouraged Jimmy to execute a 'free slap' around my face while they held my arms.

When Jimmy and his mum finally left, I caught him smuggling about fifteen of my *Star Wars* figures out of the house in his bag.

'Give me them back, you thief!' I said. Jimmy started to cry.

'Don't be so mean!' my mum chastised. 'Let him have the figures, you've got loads of others!' Like they were spares! The whole point was that you had to try and collect every individual character from all the *Star Wars* movies. I couldn't afford to just give fifteen away! That act of enforced charity set my collection back by about three years. Boba Fett, Luke in his Bespin Fatigues, C3PO with removable limbs, the Imperial Storm Trooper in Hoth battle gear – that little shit waltzed out with some of my most prized assets.

A few months later some bloke we knew got slung out of his flat for not paying the rent. Suffice to say, he wound up kipping on our sofa for about a year. He'd turned up with three carrier bags of clothes and a fat tortoiseshell cat. Only it turned out to be not fat but pregnant. Our house was already overrun with pets – we had two cats and a dog of our own that seemed to be forever spewing out litters of offspring. So when the lodger's cat gave birth to six kittens, no one was best pleased. Anyway, we must have made him feel pretty guilty about it because one night he drowned them all in a bucket of water in our front room. My brother caught him at it while he was going downstairs for a glass of water. Using our broom to hold the little blighters down, he was. He'd turned the volume right up on the telly to try and drown out their terrified meows. It being the middle of the night, *The Hitman and Her* happened to be the only thing on. The last sound those cats would have heard was something like 'Boys, Boys, Boys', by Sabrina. I don't care if you're man or beast; no one deserves that kind of undignified send-off.

To my brothers and their friends our home was a truancy safe house in which they could doss on weekday afternoons with impunity, whiling away the hours with solvent abuse and marathon sessions on our Atari games system. Three or four times a month I'd pretend to be ill in order to get out of school. Mum couldn't afford to take the day off to look after me, so usually all three of my brothers would volunteer to stay home and make sure I didn't drink any bleach or anything. Rather than have to choose which one got the nod, my mum would invariably let all three of them stay home just to keep the peace.

My pointless days around the house would be measured out by episodes of *The Sullivans*, *Sons and Daughters*, *Crown Court* and *Falcon Crest*. I'd watch anything and everything, me, even the test card. My brothers and their mates would only bother me sporadically. Sometimes their respective groups of friends would all come round at once, and a fight would break out between them. I remember having a particularly enjoyable episode of *The Waltons* interrupted by a disagreement between my youngest brother and the friend of one of my older siblings. Things got physical and my brother produced a knife from his back pocket. It was just a craft knife really – the sort where you had to push the tiny blade out of the plastic handle with a little button. Even as an eight-year-old, unseasoned in the mechanics of street fighting, I could see it was a pretty pathetic weapon. He wafted it half-heartedly at his assailant, making unconvincing threats to 'carve him up' before the whole daft fracas was broken up and I got back to watching Jim-Bob trying to cop off with Aimee Godsey.

Soon they graduated to more elaborate weaponry. One afternoon they got hold of a Gat gun, which fired lead pellets out of a spring-loaded barrel. They accidentally shot a light switch, causing it to explode and leave large scorch marks on one of the bedroom walls.

'When Mum gets home, tell her you did it,' they told me.

'What with, the gun?' I asked.'No you dickhead. Not the gun. She mustn't know about the gun.'

'Well, with what then?' I asked.

They looked at the damaged light fitting for a moment and stroked their chins.

'A hammer,' said one. 'Tell her you were playing with a hammer and accidentally smashed the light switch to pieces.'

'Until it exploded?' I asked sceptically.

'Yes!' they said angrily. 'Until it exploded!'

'I dunno,' I said, shaking my head and regarding the damage. 'It doesn't look like it's been smashed with a hammer. It looks like it's been shot with a gun.'

One of them grabbed me by the face. 'Look, you little bastard. I don't care what you think it looks like. Just tell Mum your story and stick to it.'

Suddenly the other brother came over all good-cop and intervened. 'Look, if you do this, we'll get you a toy,' he said. 'Any toy you like.'

I knew the story was unconvincing. I knew I'd get into trouble. But the deal was appealing. I'd had my eye on an Action Man with Deep Sea Diving Kit in the Argos catalogue for months. I told them my price.

'Fine,' said good cop, perusing the catalogue I'd just handed him. 'Deep Sea Diving Action Man. Good choice. It's yours come the weekend.'

When my mum came home and saw the damage to the wall, I took the blame. It was the first and last time I'd ever take the rap for a blag I hadn't done. She went berserk. Not so much about the damage to the wall but at the insulting nature of our flimsy explanation.

'You expect me to believe that?!' she shouted. 'We haven't even got a fucking hammer!' I looked around for help, but by that time my brothers had scurried out the front door.

The point I'm trying to make is, I grew up in a house where there was simply too much going on and too many people coming in and out all the time. Chaos and uncertainty reigned. Anxiety and menace hung in the air. People nicked your *Star Wars* figures and got away with it. I felt loved and reasonably safe but never that relaxed. Boo-hoo. Poor me. A nasty man drowned some cats in my front room. Hardly the stuff of a half-decent misery memoir, is it? Well, my traumas may be lame, but at least I'm not making them up.

'They still owe me that Deep Sea Diving Action Man, the tight bastards,' I think to myself angrily as I lie in bed twenty-five years later, still wide awake and staring at the ceiling. 'I bet Argos don't even do them any more. Well, they'll just have to find a vintage one off eBay instead. Some nerd will probably charge them a hundred quid for it these days. They could have got it for about a tenner back then. So who's the mug? Me or them?'

The bedroom still smells of paint and fresh carpet. There are empty boxes of flat-pack furniture stacked neatly in the corner. Each of the electrical sockets is covered with little glowing plugs with pictures of bunny rabbits on them. These are the last-minute refinements I've been making in time for the baby's arrival. This household will be a neat, tidy, quiet and hopefully slightly boring place to grow up in. I'm not quite responsible enough to make too many guarantees to my unborn offspring just yet, but I can promise that it will never be woken in the night by an act of cat murder. And, what with the precautions I've made, I also feel pretty confident that it will never be allowed to electrocute itself in one of the plug sockets. It's not much of a fatherhood manifesto but it's the best I can do right now: no cat killing, no electrocutions. And absolutely no one kipping on our sofa for more than one night at a time.

Solitude: that's what I want from my new life in this house. Don't get me wrong: I'm all for neighbourliness. If you live within three doors of me, then by all means come on over, put your feet up, have a cup of tea, help yourself to a Mr Kipling and spend some time admiring my impressive array of fashionable compact discs. Just make sure you've got an invite and it's all arranged in advance. Don't surprise me with an impromptu visit or I'm liable to blind you with the can of Mace I keep by the door for security purposes. It won't be my fault either: when unidentified visitors turn up on my doorstep, I'm afraid I follow a strict policy of spray first, ask questions later.

It's later in the day, and my wife is out front sorting out the recycling bins: paper, plastic, glass, flakes of skin, dust, unwanted Savage Garden CDs. There's a separate bin for everything these days. Whatever happened to loading all your rubbish into a stolen supermarket trolley and pushing it into the canal? Progress, I suppose.

Suddenly she waltzes into the house with a friend in tow. An unexpected, off-the-cuff, 'I-was-just-passing-and-thought-I'd-pop-by-and-say-hello' sort of a friend. The worst sort.

'You remember Flo, don't you?' she beams. Flo waves at me soppily over my wife's shoulder. I don't remember her, but she is just pretty enough for me to wish I wasn't sitting in front of the racing from Aintree while idly scratching my testicles. I emit a phlegmy cough by means of a greeting and splutter Rich Tea biscuit crumbs down my front.

See what I mean? No good can come from a house that's got too much of a welcoming air about it. Apart from anything else, I would have prepared myself better had I known Flo was going to make an appearance. I would probably have been back out in the garden with my tools. And not just the hammer and pliers either – the spirit level and Stanley knife would have made an appearance too. I might even have donned the tool belt. At the very least, I would have made sure I was munching on biscuits rather more sophisticated than boring old Rich Teas. Something like shortbread fingers I'd imagine. In any case, welcoming the likes of Flo in with such breezy spontaneity is a slippery slope. Before we know it she'll have made herself up a little bed on the sofa and be insisting that we watch *The X Factor* on Saturday night instead of *Strictly Come Dancing*.

'You're just the thin end of the wedge,' I mutter

under my breath, as she and my wife totter into the kitchen.

'What was that?' smiles Flo.

'Oh,' I splutter, 'I said d'you wanna Rich Tea?'

8
PLAYBOY

Luckily, I have some proper friends who live round here who I can meet up with under more controlled circumstances. Like Dave, who, I suppose, is kind of like my best mate. I've known him since school, was best man at his wedding and am godfather to his five-month-old daughter.

Dave and I are in his local pub. I suppose it's now my local pub too. Having a local pub already sounds like a step in the right direction towards sensible fatherly behaviour. While my current tendency towards long periods of abstinence punctuated by catastrophic bouts of binge drinking is deemed by society to be immature and stupid, the sort of inoffensive alcoholism that suburban dads cultivate nightly in pubs like this is still considered a wholly grown-up and somehow cosy form of addiction. It's one I intend to experiment with over the coming months.

'What are you drinking?' I ask Dave.

'I dunno. What are you drinking?' he replies.

This is what conversations with him are like. He can't make a decision without first knowing what you're going to do.

He's the anxious type. Always biting his nails and

thinking the sky might fall in on us at any moment. Dave sees the glass neither as half-empty nor half-full; he sees it as a potential health hazard that is likely to get tipped over on to some exposed wiring at any moment, causing a massive electrical fire in which we shall all be engulfed in flames and quickly reduced to charred, screaming corpses like those ones at the end of *Raiders of the Lost Ark*.

'Do you want any crisps?' I ask Dave.

'I dunno. Do *you* want any crisps?' he replies.

There's something else you should know about Dave: his name isn't really Dave. He wouldn't like it if I committed his actual name to print. This despite the fact that his real name is as generic and innocuous as the phoney one I've selected for him. And despite the fact that you wouldn't know or care who the hell he was even if I published his entire name, address, social security number and a small illustration of his face. I don't even have anything particularly unkind or incriminating to write about him either. But, like I say, he's the anxious type – and just a little paranoid too. He already thinks the government are trying to steal his thoughts. Imagine if his real name got used in a book. Then he'd know they were on to him. He'd probably buy a shotgun, run off into the hills and wind up blowing his own brains out. I don't want that kind of blood on my hands.

So I've decided to call him Dave. Just so you know, I am changing most other people's names in this book too. All I can guarantee is that my name really is Sam Delaney. But, for the record, if I were to use a pseudonym, it would probably be Thunderhawk Jones. Or Ricardo St Tropez.

Anyway, here we are in the pub. The very pub in which Dave first convinced me to move to the area. I told him all the worries I had about my fatherly credentials. About how I thought it was time for a calmer, more austere, more predictable way of life. I looked around at the roaring fire, approachable bar staff, dozing canines and bunch of retro old crap hanging from the walls of his local and said, 'I need to move to the suburbs.'

For once, he was unequivocal in his response.

'You wanna live where I live, mate,' he said before the words were barely out of my gob.

This is what all blokes say when you tell them you're thinking of moving. That's because most blokes think that giving sage advice just means telling people to make the exact same decisions as they have made. Even if they spend most of their time moaning about the decisions they have made.

Conversations between blokes usually go something like this:

BLOKE: I wish I'd never bought that motor. It's uncomfortable, the boot space is rubbish, it's always breaking down and it drinks petrol like nobody's business. Plus, it looks like something a bleeding hairdresser would drive.

BLOKE'S MATE: Yeah, I know what you mean. I'm thinking of getting a new car myself.

BLOKE: Are you? You wanna get what I drive, mate.

BLOKE'S MATE: But weren't you just saying how much you hated your car?

BLOKE: Well, yeah, but what else are you gonna get?

BLOKE'S MATE: I dunno, I was thinking of a Saab.

BLOKE: A Saab? A Saaaaab? What are you? A dentist from Sweden?

BLOKE'S MATE: Erm, no.

BLOKE: Some sort of architect called Steven who listens to Coldplay?

BLOKE'S MATE: No, I'm not that either.

BLOKE: Well what are you getting a Saab for then?

BLOKE'S MATE: I didn't say I was getting a Saab . . . I just said I was thinking about it.

BLOKE: Well, are you still thinking about it now I've told you what sort of people drive Saabs?

BLOKE'S MATE: [staring hollow-eyed at his pint glass and muttering sheepishly] No.

BLOKE: So what are you thinking of getting instead?

BLOKE'S MATE: [hanging his head, utterly defeated] The same car as you drive.

BLOKE: Good. That's that sorted then. Now, what are you drinking? Same as me?

We talk like this because we are confused and baffled by the incessant challenges life spews up. Each and every day a man is faced by difficult questions like 'What mortgage?' 'What car?' 'What sandwich filling?' 'What mid-price pair of smart casual trousers?' and other dilemmas that sound like titles of helpful magazines. In fact, I think the first two already are titles of helpful magazines. The second two aren't but should be and, should any shrewd magazine publishers reading this agree, then may I be the first to throw my hat in the ring for the role of editor-in-chief on either publication. Particularly the one about sandwiches.

Anyway, none of us knows how to answer these important questions with any degree of certainty or confidence. We can never be sure that we have made the right choice about anything. Our only means of judging our decisions is to compare them with those of our peers. By subtly bullying our peers into making the same decisions as us we can feel slightly more comfortable about our ridiculous, transient and ultimately futile existences. All of our fates are pretty much in the hands of outrageous fortune or the Gods or The Power of Greyskull or whatever you want to call it. We have control over so little – but we can sometimes maliciously influence the decisions of our best mates for no other reason than our own petty-minded sense of self-satisfaction.

So, in a way, we're all like Dave.

'Becoming a dad is . . . a journey,' he'd told me that night in the pub, gingerly placing his pint on the table and affecting a faraway look in his eyes. 'It's like discovering what life is really about. I'm suddenly, like, "What have I been *doing* all these years? Life's not about drinking and drugs and, y'know . . . French electronic dance music."' Yeah, I know, I found that last example strange too, but I let it pass. 'It's about *human beings*! I mean, I look at my little girl's face in the morning and everything is in perspective.'

I nodded politely. But inside my head I thought: 'That's funny. It's not like Dave to speak in a series of meaningless clichés. Maybe those meaningless clichés are in fact true, that's why people say them all the time.'

Next he started going on about the area like some sort of crappy, half-pissed estate agent.

'The schools are great, the pubs are great and the transport links to town are plentiful!' he slurred.

Ordinarily, I don't like 'transport links' as a term or a concept. And on this occasion I found his strange use of the word 'plentiful' a bit disconcerting too. But I nevertheless noticed myself treating his words with slightly less disdain than they perhaps deserved. I never thought there'd be a day when the quality of local schools or even pubs would be factors in my assessment of an area. If anything, I would have actively sought out areas with rubbish schools and disgusting pubs just to make a point.

'Just how disgusting are the pubs round here?' I would ask the estate agent.

'Oh, they're truly disgusting, sir. Full of murderers and racists with rude words smeared out in human faeces all over the walls!' would come the reply. Or at least it would have done, had the estate agent had his head screwed on.

'What about the schools?' I would venture.

'Piss-poor. Not one pupil has ever passed so much as a spelling test, and the teachers are all paedos.'

'Great! Where do I sign?'

But my mindset was clearly altering. Sitting in the pub listening to Dave drone on about the mundane appeal of his locality, his words began to sound strangely appealing. It was like I was one of those world leaders you see sitting in the middle of an international summit. Someone had stuck a special pair of headphones on my ears that helpfully translated all the seemingly meaningless foreign babble into a semi-coherent form. I had seen the light. No, that doesn't sound right. I had seen the darkness? No, what I had seen was the dimly lit greyness of suburban family life. And I quite liked it.

So I convinced my wife that we should move here. And now I'm back in the same pub drinking the same beer and eating the same flavour crisps as Dave. The baby is due in a couple of weeks. Dave is giving me some last-minute advice on the matter.

'Mate, these are the most important two weeks of your life', he says.

'I know. Buying nappies, getting the birth bag ready, planning the route to the hospital,' I reply.

'No, mate. Fuck all that,' he says fixing me with a grim stare. His eyes are baggy and his face unshaven. He has been outside for a fag about eighteen times already. We've only been here three-quarters of an hour. 'You've got to understand that having a baby ruins your life. So you have to squeeze as much living in now before it's too late.'

I look at Dave's mad face. His right eye twitches manically. He needs more sleep. I think about what he's said. Have I really done enough living over the past thirty-two years? Depends on what he means by 'living'. If he means travelling to the farthest reaches of the globe, meeting strange and fascinating people, enriching my soul, invigorating my mind, witnessing the extremes of nature in all its many guises, unlocking the secrets of the human condition and discovering the whispered truths of the universe, then the answer is undoubtedly no. Mind you, me and the missus had a great weekend in Rome last year. Went right to the top of the bloody great tower at the Vatican we did. The staircase was steep and windy and my wife started to go all dizzy, so we didn't stop for long. But for the brief few moments we were up there I remember looking out across the majesty of all those stunning buildings and thinking, 'Blimey, what an achievement. I could never make something as good as this. No patience. Never even finished so much as an Airfix Spitfire model without getting distracted. But of course, I don't believe in God. Maybe if I did I'd have had more of an incentive to finish that rotten Spitfire. Would a plastic rendition of a Second World War fighter plane be an appropriate tribute to a deity? Probably not. If anything, He might find it a crude and offensive reminder of man's tendency towards self-destruction. I would probably incur his mighty wrath and be struck down with righteous fury. Or something. So, all things considered, probably best I stick to being a Godless heathen after all.' It was probably the most profound thought world travel had ever inspired in me. By the time I'd finished having it, we were back at the bottom of the steps buying overpriced Cornettos from a street vendor.

Personally, I don't see why the notion of enlightened, fulfilling, wholehearted living is always associated with travel. In particular, it seems to be associated with doing outlandish outdoor activities in places like New Zealand or Wales. There's a couple of idiots who live down my street – outdoorsy types they are – who have got a bumper sticker on their Land Rover that says 'One Life, Live It'. Well, what else are we gonna do with it? Lick it? Frame it? Buy it a kebab? I know what they're really trying to say with their stupid sticker. They're trying to say that you should get outdoors and climb up a rock. Or piss about inside a cave wearing a helmet with a light on it. Or buy a mountain bike. The implication is that, unless you're spending at least fifty quid a month in Millets on Gore-Tex-based outdoor wear, then you're pissing your life up the wall. Which strikes me as a bit narrow-minded. I mean, I've done my fair share of adventure sports, and I can't say it taught me much about the meaning of life. In the summer of 1984 I attended Camp Dolphin Adventure Camp in Wales with my mate Alex. We did rock climbing, abseiling, potholing, kayaking, the lot. I spent the week making a bit of a prick out of myself if I'm honest. I'm just not cut out for that sort of thing. The instructor fined us a Lion bar every time we used our knees for support during rock climbing. I was the poor bastard who owed him twenty-five Lion bars by the end of the week. I blew my entire tuck budget on that idiot. Sums up the sort of fascistic mentality of the people who go in for that sort of outward-bound crap if you ask me. I mean, OK, I admit it: I'm not that good at extreme sports. I'm not a particularly co-ordinated sort of a bloke. Does that mean that I am unable to make the most out of life? Just because I can't climb a rock without using my knees? Is that what those Land-Rover-driving bastards up the street reckon? Well, screw them and screw their sleeveless, Gore-Tex jackets too.

In any case, none of that matters because that sort of stuff isn't what Dave means by 'living'.

When Dave says that I should cram as much 'living' as possible into the next two weeks, he means I should cram as much 'drinking' as possible into the next two weeks. Maybe throw in a bit of drunken leering at girls for good measure. Spend a couple of soul-corroding evenings in a lap-dancing bar. Perhaps nip into the bogs once in a while to shovel drugs up my nose off the edge of my Oyster card. That's the kind of living he's got in mind. Because that's the kind of living he misses from his carefree childless days. Of course, the irony is, he didn't really spend much time doing any of those things during his carefree childless days. But at least he always had the option of doing them. That option has now been removed. Not by his wife but by himself. He's responsible enough to know, deep down, that's no way for a decent adult to behave. But it suits his inner narrative, his carefully constructed self-mythology, to pretend that he's some sort of rampant hedonist who's having his rock 'n' roll instincts cruelly restrained by the chains of domesticity. Like many blokes, Dave likes to think of himself as some kind of maverick Lizard King living on the edge of reason and decency. He usually thinks these thoughts while trimming his front hedges on a Sunday morning, listening to Elaine Page's Radio 2 show on his transistor radio. The mundane truth, which he can't bring himself to confront, is that he's actually a good, honest husband and father.

This is a form of self-delusion I must take care to avoid. Hard times lie ahead. Parenthood won't be a walk in the park. But I've gone into this with my eyes wide open. I can't allow myself to start thinking that a life of buttoned-down responsibility has been somehow imposed on me. That way madness lies: I just have to look at Dave's right eye to realise that.

Anyway, I figure I've done my fair share of mindless, low-rent hedonism. Over the years I've spent three separate Friday nights in three separate A&E wards across

London. I've wet myself in a coffee shop in Amsterdam. I've bought drugs off a Hispanic gangster in New York who threw me out of his moving Cadillac. Only the other month I got slung off a train in Stevenage for nicking a miniature bottle of gin from the buffet car. Oh yeah, I've lived life on the edge all right. I even attended a party at the *Playboy* mansion once. I was in LA on an assignment for a magazine and somehow wangled an invite to some daft party Hugh Hefner was throwing. It wasn't all that, to be honest. The snacks were dry and boring, the beer was watery and the bunnies' conversational skills were nothing short of pathetic. Their smiles were sparkly, their bosoms heaving, but their eyes were cold and dead. I know it may sound strange, but they seemed somehow indifferent, as if they wished they weren't talking to me and the other idiots who were slouched around the place but were far away with someone else. Or maybe they were simply wishing they were dead. Who knows? Suffice to say, I've been to the edge of reason and decency, and it wasn't all it's cracked up to be.

On the other hand, if Dave is simply pointing out that I'll have no spare time left once I'm a dad, then good. I hate spare time. Makes me itchy and irritable. Once I've finished work, had my tea, done the washing up and watched a DVD, I'm usually stumped about what to do next. I find myself staring out the window at the neighbourhood cats, doing weird cat voices like Johnny Morris. It's boring. One of the main reasons I'm having a kid is to eat up all that spare time. I won't be telling Dave this, though. He loves spare time. It would break his heart to know my feelings on the matter.

I drain my pint and put my hand on his shoulder. 'Don't worry, Dave,' I say softly, 'I'm gonna spend the next fortnight getting absolutely twatted.'

He looks up, doe-eyed. 'Thanks, mate,' he says. 'That means a lot.'

9

QUINCY

I'm pulling some blue surgical scrubs over my Levis and thinking that I look a bit like Doogie Howser MD. I am in a tiny side-room off the main corridor in the maternity ward. It seems that this is where the doctors and nurses leave their personal belongings and civilian clothes during the working day. I am surrounded by their handbags and wallets. There are iPods and mobile phones strewn about the place. They're not very security conscious, these people. This being Britain's poshest NHS hospital, maybe they're confident that no one is likely to thieve from them. They are wrong. 'If I stole those now, I'd get away with it easy,' I reason with myself. 'Nobody would ever suspect an expectant father whose wife has just been rushed into the emergency delivery room to have taken the time to go thieving. Even if they did suspect, they'd probably be too polite to actually bring it up. In the midst of a personal trauma like this, no one's gonna have the guts to accuse me of stealing a pink iPod mini from a trainee obstetrician.'

It's not usual for me to thieve, but extreme circumstances can make you do strange things. Like those people trapped in car wreckages who start to have sex with each other amid the twisted metal and broken glass. It's a distraction technique to keep the mind from dwelling on the pain and fear. Maybe I'm subconsciously hoping to get caught and arrested and dragged down the nick, thus avoiding attendance at a birth that is rapidly spiralling out of control. Whatever my subliminal reasons are, it's definitely out of character for me to nick stuff – I'm simply too gutless.

A nurse pops her head around the door and says my wife has been asking for me. I drop the wallet and pull on the silly blue surgical hat they've given me. I feel like I'm about to start a shift on the deli counter at Morrison's. My hands are shaking a bit. I clock my reflection in the window and decide that, in this light, I look more like Quincy than Doogie Howser. Emboldened, I take a deep breath and stride out of the locker room to face my destiny.

We've already been here fourteen hours. Fourteen hours of labour. Sounds scary, doesn't it? Makes you imagine fourteen hours of incessant agony and screaming, hot towels, bucketloads of blood, legions of panicked midwives, shouty doctors, bleeping machines and stirrups. That's how they portray it on the box. That's also how other dads will describe it to you in a bid to make you shit yourself. Every dad I know has told me some sort of petrifying tale of delivery-room woe over the past nine months. Not one of them has tried to reassure me that some births actually do pass without notable incident. That's because messy-birth stories are the modern man's equivalent to war stories.

The modern man has generally led a life devoid of action, danger and peril. While his ancestors fought in the

Somme or spent five years in a Japanese POW camp getting repeatedly jabbed with a spiky piece of bamboo through the bars of his cage, the modern man just drifts through life moaning about the price of petrol and the inadequate speed of his broadband connection. Our lives are a pathetic series of namby-pamby concerns and rubbish, self-indulgent whinging. This book alone should have already given you an accurate impression of just how inconsequential the preoccupations of the twenty-first-century Western male truly are. The closest any of us ever gets to raw, undiluted terror is in the delivery room. So it's little wonder we milk those moments for anecdotes until they're bone-dry. It's the source of constant exaggeration and one-upmanship within inter-male conversations.

'We were in there for the best part of a week,' one might say to another over a pint. 'My missus was losing a litre of blood per minute. Two midwives dropped dead from exhaustion right in front of us. In the end they had to cut the baby out of my wife's bumhole. It was the only possible exit point apparently.'

'Well, that's nothing,' another will retort. 'They ran out of drugs in our hospital, so I had to nip out to Threshers and buy my missus a bottle of Teacher's whisky to swig while they amputated her legs, which had become infected with MRSA during the first of three abortive caesarean attempts. In the end she died.'

'But I saw her earlier this morning. She looked fine.'

'Oh yeah, she's alive now. But she was technically dead for eighteen minutes. They had to jump-start her heart using one of those special machines with the electric blasters.'

So late last night, after my wife had woken me up and explained that her waters had broken, I was expecting the worst. I drove bleary-eyed to the hospital and checked her in. They stuck us in a nice, softly lit maternity room and said the midwife would be in to see us soon. My wife popped herself up on the bed and we started to wait.

'What are you staring at?' she asked me after a few silent moments had passed.

'You,' I said. 'Are you sure your waters have broken?'

'Of course I'm sure,' she said. 'Why?'

'Well, you don't seem to have gone into labour yet.'

'Oh really? How can you tell?'

'Well, you should really be screaming by now. And sweating. And telling me to fuck off and that.'

'OK then: fuck off.'

'Yeah, like that but more shouty and mad . . .'

'No, I really mean it. Fuck off.'

So I fucked off. The lady from the ante-natal classes said I should do whatever my missus says during labour. Mind you, I was beginning to question the credibility of those ante-natal classes. I mean, they told me about the blood and the pain and the tears. They told me about the need to bring along light, nutritious snacks such as trail bars and dried fruit. (I forgot to buy these and so ended up throwing half a box of After Eights and a Babybel into the birthing bag on the way out the door.) They suggested I bring some iPod speakers through which to play the soothing sounds of Enya or Clannad. (Again I forgot these, but I am not averse to the idea of having a stab at 'Orinoco Flow' myself, should the situation demand it.) They even went as far as to warn me that my wife might actually shit herself before my very eyes. But they didn't say anything about the boredom, about the long, tedious hours in which you just sit around waiting for the real action to start.

'So, how are you finding labour so far?' I asked her as I re-entered the room, having had a little walk around the ward to let her calm down. This was supposed to show her that I'd now accepted that she really was in the early stage of childbirth. But I must have misjudged it in some way because she just told me to shut my 'fucking mouth'.

Which only reconfirmed to me that she was in labour. She had not yet got on to pushing, heaving, thrashing or crying. In fact, she still had her jeans on. There were certainly no signs of a baby – she hadn't so much as shat herself yet. But it was unlike her to be quite so sweary towards me, so I was prepared to take her word for it when she said she was experiencing regular contractions. She has always had an intimidatingly high pain threshold. I find it emasculating, if I'm honest. I'll get a paper cut from opening an envelope and yelp like I've been smashed in the face with a broken beer glass. She drops an iron on her foot and winces like she's just stubbed her toe.

'How regular are the contractions?' I asked her.

'About once every ten minutes,' she said. 'I'm actually having one right now.' Then she kind of flinched in the same way I do when I nick myself shaving.

The first few hours tick-tocked by without anything much happening. Occasionally someone came in and took her blood pressure. I kept asking questions about the 'diameter of the contraction' in a bid to sound knowledgeable and interested. I didn't really know what any of it meant: I was just regurgitating any old phrases I could remember from the gigantic *Guide to Childbirth* that I'd found next to our bed a few weeks earlier. Everyone ignored me anyway. I almost began to wish that I'd brought a book with me. Or some cards, a set of Travel Yahtzee, some felt tips and a colouring book. Once we ran out of conversation, the atmosphere became slightly awkward, to be honest. Mostly I just sat there holding my wife's hand and trying to adopt a sympathetic but calm facial expression. I'm no good at doing that sort of thing though; my face lacks the subtle nuance of the accomplished thespian. So I wound up sitting there with this weird furrowed brow and exaggerated pout, like Gary Coleman in *Diff'rent Strokes*.

In the end I actually fell asleep on the floor. One of the nurses, sensing that my slightly imbecilic demeanour might prove a liability during the lengthy birthing process, made me up a little bed on the floor with a camping mattress. I screwed the hood of my sweatshirt tight around my face and drifted quickly into a shallow sleep, punctuated by a series of horrifying apparitions. First I dreamed that the doctors were rummaging around my wife's innards unable to find the baby; then I dreamed that they found the baby, but that it had a dog's head. Next, I dreamed that the baby was born with my face, complete with stubble and receding hairline, and was pointing and laughing at me manically as it left the womb. Finally I dreamed that my mother was in the room, urging the doctors to have me ejected. 'Don't let clumsy watch,' she was saying. 'He'll only trip over one of the machines and ruin everything.'

My gangly lack of co-ordination is a source of constant amusement and concern to my mother. I once fell down the stairs in my dressing gown when I was about fifteen, exposing my flapping genitals to some friends she'd invited round for coffee. Another time, when I was babysitting for one of my nieces, I slipped on some wet grass in the park and kicked her face down into a paddling pool. Some other mums rushed over and fished her out, shooting me horrified scowls and refusing to let me have her back.

'She's my niece!' I explained. 'Give her to me!' They just ignored me.

'Don't worry,' they comforted the wailing child. 'We won't let the nasty man hurt you.' It was like a kidnapping. They only agreed to hand her over once I'd shown them ID to prove that I was a relative and not just a mad teenage bastard who walked round parks trying to drown toddlers.

These are the regrettable incidents around which my mother has chosen to define my entire persona. Trouble is, this cruel and superficial caricature she has created has started to govern my own sense of self. As I drifted in and out of consciousness on that hospital floor, my mother's disembodied cackling echoed through my mind and I began to fret uncontrollably about my physical ability to father a child. Never mind the question marks that still hung over my mental, emotional and spiritual capabilities – I was now questioning my body's ability to perform basic childcare tasks. Would I be able to even hold this infant without tripping over my own feet and dropping it down a flight of stairs? Would I squish its delicate innards with my ungainly and brutish hands? Maybe I was the sort of useless incompetent who ends up on the front page of the paper having accidentally trapped his baby's hands in the George Foreman Grilling Machine while trying to make a tuna melt. There I'd be, looking all guilty on the front page of *The Sun* below a headline that read 'Evil Twat Toasts Baby'. The humiliation of it! I mean, I don't think I'm that much of a twat, but nobody does until they actually wind up toasting a baby. Then they think, 'Oh no! I've accidentally toasted the baby! Hopefully people will realise that I'm not evil, just clumsy!' But by that stage it's too late; the papers have got hold of the story and the public are drawing their own conclusions. You're vilified across national news media, people call radio phone-ins to demand that the government have you chemically castrated and you end up hiring Max Clifford for a million quid that you haven't got. But not even he can save you, and you wind up having to live under an assumed name and get facial surgery like a former mob henchman turned FBI informant, only much less exciting and glamorous. The further this baby crept from the womb, the more pronounced my anxieties became.

I was suddenly awake but remained still on the floor with my eyes shut. My heart was pounding and my brain throbbed with worry. I sensed a commotion in the room. For just a few moments I considered continuing to feign sleep until the whole thing was over and done with. Perhaps I could pretend to be dead. Then the midwife accidentally kicked me in the shin and I sprang up like a meerkat.

'I think I nodded off!' I said, bewildered.

'You've been asleep for two hours,' my wife replied dismissively. I glanced outside and noticed that morning had broken. My wife was in a bumless gown and had tubes and wires attached to her.

'What's happening now?' I asked.

'We're about to administer the epidural,' said a male nurse clutching a massive syringe.

'I thought we were going to talk about that first . . . I mean, weren't you only gonna have that if it got unbearably painful?' I said.

'It is unbearably painful,' my wife deadpanned.

Then they shot a nuclear dose of painkilling drugs into her spine and everyone drifted out of the room.

At least we were now approaching the sort of heightened state of drama everyone had led me to expect. The midwife who had guided us calmly and sympathetically through the night finished her shift and was replaced by someone who seemed rather less smart and charming. She shambled into the room, barely introduced herself and tucked into a packet of Dairylea Dunkers beside the bed.

'I haven't had my breakfast,' she explained with her mouth full. She didn't instil much confidence in me. If she applied the same slapdash approach to midwifery as she did to her own personal nutrition then we were all in trouble. The contractions started to come quicker.

'PUSH! PUSH!' the midwife shouted in my wife's face, spitting crumbs of Dunker everywhere. Then, as soon as the pain receded, she would slump back into her chair, returning her attentions to the vacuous chit-chat she'd been sharing with a student doc who'd come along to watch.

'I always laugh when I hear about these celebrities who are too posh to push,' she droned. 'Like Merr-derna. Merr-derna has had all her kids with a caesarean. But what makes Merr-derna more special than anyone else?'

'Is she talking about Madonna? How could she not know how to say the name properly?' I thought to myself angrily. 'She must be doing it on purpose to annoy me.' I became fixated by the issue. Suddenly it was the only sound my brain could register: 'Merr-derna, Merr-derna, Merr-derna.' With the tension and the hot August sun shining in my face I eventually snapped.

'MADONNA!' I shouted. 'YOU MEAN MADONNA!'

'I know, that's what I said!' she barked back at me. 'Merr-derna. I know who I mean!'

'But why are you saying it like that?'

'Like what?'

'With "er"s instead of "a"s? How could you not know how to say her name properly? She's the most famous person on the planet! The pronunciation is commonly recognised to be MA-DONN-A! It's not like "potato" or "tomato" or "garage"! It's not open to debate!'

'I don't like your tone,' she said in a manner she'd clearly been trained to employ with problem patients.

'What's going on?' said an important-looking lady doctor striding through the door.

'You're a doctor – you'll know!' I said. 'Is it Merr-derna or Madonna?'

She ignored me and began to take a concerned look between my wife's thighs. 'Right, we've waited long enough for this baby,' she said. 'We're getting it out right now – take her into the delivery room.'

Nurses arrived and quickened their pace as they started to wheel my wife's bed out of the door and into a room across the hall full of elaborate Heath Robinson-style devices. The doctor explained that the baby might be starting to panic. And if the baby started to panic, it might shit itself. And if it shat itself, it might swallow its own shit and get brain-damaged. So they'd have to cut it out right away to prevent all that from happening. Then she sent me into that little side-room to put my scrubs on.

And now I'm in my scrubs and shuffling into the delivery room preparing to face my destiny. 'Life – funny old business really, isn't it?' I think to myself. 'You drift along getting born, learning to use the potty, going to school, then going to work, having a girlfriend, going for a nice walk in the park once in a while, sometimes getting the odd parking ticket. You have it off, you get a bit drunk, you watch telly. You get a stabbing pain in your chest and convince yourself it's a heart attack, then call NHS Direct and they tell you it's just wind. You think thoughts, you hear noises, you wonder where to go on holiday. Sometimes you inexplicably find yourself smelling your own hand. Yep, it might have its ups and downs but, generally speaking, it seems to jog along fairly predictably. You get to thirty-two and think you've seen it all. And then you're in a hospital and your wife, the person you've kind of based all your assumptions about the next sixty years of your life on, is lying on a bed with loads of doctors and nurses setting about her with machines, looking like she might easily cark it any minute now. Meanwhile, your unborn child is inside her tummy possibly bingeing on its own shit. Anything could happen in the next couple of minutes. *Anything*. My life could be turned on its head. I will not become a decent family man in a warm friendly house with a loving wife and child. I will be a heartbroken wreck living in a bed-sit drinking Malibu from a teacup and wishing I was dead. Up until this point the most dramatic thing that had ever happened to me was getting briefly stuck under a lilo at White City swimming baths in 1984. For a few seconds I thought I was drowning. Then I just kind of broke free and carried on playing. I guess I thought it'd never get any worse than that. If anything goes wrong now, I'm not sure I've got the strength to deal with it.'

I survey the room. The fussing medics. The bowls of what looks like offal but may well be my wife's pancreas and spleen. My wife looks up at me with an expression that seems to plead for reassurance. 'No good looking at me,' I think. 'I'm in a worse state than you. I mean, at least you've got all those lovely spine drugs numbing your brain. Me, I'm flying solo.' Nevertheless, I try to give her my best look of reassurance. I think it comes out like the Gary Coleman face again, but she doesn't seem to mind. She's battered.

'Push! Push!' the assembled maternity team shout in unison. They encourage me to join in. I feel all self-conscious and just mumble the words meekly. 'I can see its head!' shouts someone. 'Do you want to come down and look?' they ask.

'No thanks, if it's all the same to you,' I reply.

Everyone laughs. 'For fuck's sake, my wife and child are about to die!' I think to myself. 'Forgive me if I don't want to walk down there and watch the whole messy business up close, you unfeeling bastards!'

Suddenly a baby appears. Just like that. One minute the doc is looking panicked and hopeless; the next this slippery, wrinkled human being has flopped into her arms like a wet balloon. She places it directly on my wife's chest.

'Jesus Christ!' I say, gasping for air. Nobody is dead after all. The baby is looking a bit blue, but no one seems overly concerned about that. It's probably normal, so I just don't mention it.

The medical team are cooing like it's the first time any of them has ever seen this happen.

'Can you tell what it is?' one of them asks me.

'Yeah!' I say defensively. 'It's a girl, I think!'

'That's right!' they chorus. 'It's a little girl!' I start to cry. I gingerly take the baby in my arms and brandish her under my wife's nose.

'Look, we've had a little girl!' I squeak in weird, fluctuating octaves. She's so off her tits it's hard to know if any of this is actually registering. She smiles and nods, but for all I know she thinks I've just asked her if she'd like a Toblerone and some Skips for her tea.

As more tears spew down my face, I'm filled with an overwhelming sense of pride. Pride for producing this little baby. Pride for guessing the sex right when I was put on the spot by that nurse. And perhaps most of all pride for crying real, unforced tears of sincere emotion. I don't think I've had a good cry since I lost the Subbuteo World Cup Final on my mum's kitchen table in 1988. And even that was partly due to some cat litter getting in my eyes. I shed a few tears at my grandma's funeral ten years ago but, if I'm being entirely honest, I helped them along a bit by conjuring a few extra-sad thoughts and blinking a lot. I figured it would be a bit rude not to. But these tears are different; they are 100 per cent natural, unforced and involuntary. I call them organic tears, and, as they scorch my cheeks, they feel good. I wipe them from my face with my sleeve and look down at this little girl in my arms. A mop of black hair, wrinkled skin, a bluish-grey complexion and pretty, open eyes that dart around the room. You could call her scary and weird-looking, I suppose, but I quite like her. I kiss her putty-like forehead and tell her that daddy loves her very much. And d'you know what? I actually feel like I mean it.

10

SATAN

I suppose to anybody else she may still look a bit strange. She's still got that slightly corpse-like complexion, and there's a bit of scabby umbilical cord dangling from her belly button. Plus, there's blood still smeared here and there where that effing midwife didn't wash her properly. But to me she's beautiful. I know that sounds corny, like something I feel I'm supposed to say. But you'll just have to take my word for it: that's genuinely how I feel. I'm not trying to make myself out to be any more sensitive or caring than the next bastard. I mean, falling in love with your own offspring moments after it's born is actually quite egotistical. I helped make this thing. Her nose looks a bit like mine. Of course I think she's great. Becoming infatuated with your own spawn is just about the purest form of narcissism. Actually, make that the second purest form of narcissism. The purest form of narcissism is that practised by a leading Hollywood actor, who is rumoured to be having a homosexual affair with his own professional lookalike.

People worry about failing to form a bond with their own baby. They think there'll be no chemistry. That they'll perceive the child as nothing more than a wrinkly, wailing bundle of inconvenience. But sitting in this delivery room with her in my arms, watching her big, blue, useless eyes flitter about the place trying to consume the meaningless blurry shapes that surround her, I don't think I'm going to have that problem. Admittedly, her attitude towards me has been slightly indifferent so far. But then she's only about twenty minutes old, so she probably needs more time to get to know me. Once she's heard a few of my jokes, watched me dance, heard me tell a few brilliantly imaginative and off-the-cuff bedtime stories and seen some of those amusing facial expressions I've been developing for her, I feel certain that she'll warm to me.

And once we've got that blood off her and that scabby bit of cord removed, she'll look even more gorgeous and lovable than she does already. Not that aesthetics should matter. I mean, look at *Rosemary's Baby*. That child was the spawn of the devil and yet Rosemary still learned to love it soon enough. Mia Farrow shuffles into that room full of Satanists, sees the cot covered in black velvet sheets with an upside down crucifix hanging where a Winnie the Pooh would usually be and can immediately tell that something's not quite right. Then she peers inside at the terrifying infant and can't believe her eyes.

'What have you done to it?' she asks the assembled throng of devil lovers. 'What have you done to its eyes?'

An awkward silence falls over the room. The Satanists don't know where to look. In the end one of them clears his throat and says: 'Satan is his father . . . he came up from hell and begat a son of mortal woman.'

Personally, I always thought he could have phrased that a bit better. I mean, when you're breaking bad news, you should try to be a bit gentle. Say something like 'Look, luv, there's no easy way of putting this: we drugged you then summoned up Satan and got him to have it off with you while you were unconscious. I know it sounds stupid but it seemed like a laugh at the time. Anyway, that's his kid over there. Sorry.' Employing weird biblical terms like 'begat' was always likely to make a bad situation worse. Obviously Rosemary is furious to learn that she was date-raped by Satan. But anger soon gives way to mere annoyance, which in turn gives way to involuntary maternal instinct. Within minutes she's gently rocking the demented little bastard to sleep and singing him a nice lullaby. Not that he'd probably appreciate that sort of thing, but it's the thought that counts. The point is, it doesn't matter how your child turns out, you're genetically programmed to think it's brilliant and want to take care of it and all that. Even if it has demonic eyes and a set of hoofs where its hands and feet should be. All my baby's got is an iffy complexion which in any case will probably start to look a bit healthier within the next hour or so.

Someone takes the baby from me and injects it in the foot. I don't like to ask why – I'm sure it's for the best. I'm so awestruck by what these people have just done that they could start dangling her upside down and slapping her on the arse right now and I wouldn't question them. In fact, that was the sort of thing the *Carry On* films had half-led me to expect anyway. That, and a scenario in which I accidentally slip on some afterbirth, go skating the length of the corridor and get my head stuck between the cleavage of an overbearing matron. If there's one element of disappointment to this otherwise magnificent day, it's that none of those things have actually happened.

One thing's for sure: special bonds were formed in this room today. These heroic few were the architects of my fledgling family. In fact, I now consider them to be unofficial family members themselves. I imagine that we will occasionally holiday with the obstetrician in years to come. Perhaps the anaesthetist and her husband will come over for lunch once in a while. I can't see myself getting too matey with that midwife but even she might pop round sometimes to see how we're getting on. I'll just make sure I'm out those days. None of us will ever forget this moment.

At least, that's what I'd like to think. But a few of the nurses have just ambled out of the room carrying a pile of bloodied debris. And the doctor who seemed to be in charge is now rushing into the adjacent room, where another emergency delivery seems to be under way. 'Hang on a minute,' I think to myself. 'We were the centre of everyone's universe a minute ago! I thought we were special! But we were obviously just another faceless family on your baby conveyor belt. I feel so used.'

We're moved on to a ward with loads of other mums, babies and gormless-looking dads who are standing around awkwardly, not really knowing what to do next. The uniformity of it makes me feel even less special. On reflection, ours was a fairly unexceptional birthing experience. A load of boring waiting, a sudden flurry of activity, then a strange sense of anti-climax. A great allegory for all of life's important moments really.

I am suddenly overcome with a very particular feeling and can't quite put my finger on what you might call it. A sort of yearning inside. A strangely familiar ache; a feeling of emptiness. Is it post-natal shock perhaps? Or sorrow? Regret? Panic? No, it's none of those things. Ah, that's it: it's hunger.

'I'm nipping out for a sandwich,' I tell my wife. She half-ignores me while casually breast-feeding the new-born and reading a copy of *Heat* at the same time. This starting-a-family business: it's as easy as breathing.

I swagger down the hospital corridor still dressed in my scrubs. I am so excited about everything. I carry myself like a father: with confidence, purposefulness and a touch of self-importance. I am half-hoping that, in this get-up, I may be mistaken for an actual doctor. Perhaps someone will approach me in the lift and ask my advice on their thrombosis. 'Ah yes,' I could say, stroking away at my chin. 'Thrombosis . . . tricky . . . verrrrrrry tricky.' Then, hopefully, the lift door would ping and I could just run off. Perhaps someone else might even invite me to take part in a surgical procedure. Nothing serious, like a heart bypass: that would be too dangerous. But maybe I could just help recast someone's broken arm. Or assist in a vasectomy. I could probably get away with that if I kept my mouth shut and passed the forceps whenever anyone asked.

But none of this happens. In fact, once I'm out on the street in this silly blue uniform, people just swerve to avoid me on the assumption that I'm a lunatic. I stop at a flower stall to pick up some celebratory daffs for my wife.

'New dad?' asks the burly, shaven-headed florist as he wraps them up for me.

'Yes!' I say, delighted that someone has bothered to acknowledge my new lofty status in the human race. 'I've just had a little girl!'

He looks a good fifteen years older than me. I figure he's probably got three or four littluns of his own at home. Certainly he's got a nice big gut that's befitting of a proper dad. My stomach is flat in a puny, as opposed to a cover of *Men's Health*, sort of way. How can I expect a child to respect me, looking as weak and callow as this? I'm waiting for this florist to hand me my change with a complimentary nugget of parenting advice. Maybe a tip on how to cultivate a gut something like his. What's his secret? Suet for breakfast? One of those beer hats with the straws attached? Come on, man, furnish me with your wisdom!

'Welcome to eighteen years of hell,' is all he says as he hands over the flowers and the change.

'Oh,' I say, a little confused. 'Thanks.'

He does a little shake of his head as he turns to the next customer, no doubt seeking a way in which to spoil their mood and crush their dreams in similar fashion.

'Someone's anniversary is it?' he'll say. 'Yeah, well, what's the point in celebrating another year spent ensnared in a joyless and debilitating relationship? Monogamy is unnatural, human relationships are futile and we all die in the end anyway. That'll be four pound fifty for the tulips, cheers.' Hardly bloody service with a smile, is it?

Still, it'll take more than that miserable harbinger of doom and chrysanthemums to piss on my disco. I've become well used to the jaded attitudes of parents like him over the past few months. When you first tell them you've got a baby on the way, they're all 'It's the best thing you'll ever do!' But that soon gives way to a patronising tirade of warnings about how shitty your life is about to become. 'Now you'll find out what life's really about, you naive, lazy bastard!' they seem to say. Having spent years resenting your carefree lifestyle of late nights, lie-ins and puke-free clothing, they shiver with excitement about you finally joining the ranks of baggy-eyed, moaning, knackered shitheads like them. Honestly, to listen to them you'd have thought no one had ever had to change a couple of nappies, knock up a bit of mashed banana and sing the odd nursery rhyme five or six times a day. The way they grumble about parenthood, you'd have thought it was like working in a Stalinist gulag. Something tells me it's rather less taxing than that. But what do I know? Maybe I'll see what they're on about in a couple of months' time and regret my irritatingly positive attitude to the whole thing. But for now I'm not going to let Mr Chuckles the flower man or his ilk knock me off my stride.

When I get back on to the maternity ward, I can hear another delivery turning ugly in the theatre.

'Fuuuuuckkkk! Nnnnnnoooooo!!' I can hear some poor woman screaming.

'See,' I say excitedly, nudging my wife as I hand over the daffs. 'That's the sort of thing I was expecting from you! Screaming and shouting and all that!'

She ignores me and continues to read a story about Mischa Barton's underarm sweat marks. I am suddenly overcome by a strange urge to go and interfere with what's going on in that delivery room. I creep over and try and peer through the gap in the door. A harassed-looking dad steps outside to catch his breath. It's all got too much for him. Lucky for him, I'm on hand with a comforting word or two.

'See your missus is having a bit of trouble over there,

pal,' I wink at him knowingly. He looks up at me, eyes wild and bloodshot, mouth too dry to speak.

'Shame, innit?' I continue. 'Don't worry, it'll all work itself out in a minute. What's probably happening is that your nipper's trying to eat its own shit. But they're very good this lot, they'll sort it all out for you in a jiffy.' He just keeps staring, his mouth now wide open. Poor bloke doesn't know how to thank me.

'Shame your wife's the squeamish type, mind you,' I conclude. 'Don't know if you noticed, but mine barely made a peep.' He is now walking back into the delivery room where things seem to be coming to a head.

'Anyway, be lucky!' I call after him.

That's me: wise, helpful and interfering. I'm starting to feel like a dad already.

11

BRAIN

I walk up the garden path, open the gate, put one foot on to the street and then stop. I blink. I turn my head around slowly and look back at the house. Then I turn back again and look at the street. My mouth falls open like a stupid fish. I look both ways, furrow my brow and think to myself: 'What was it I was supposed to do next?'

My brain doesn't respond. It just slouches lazily inside my skull with its feet up, smoking a fag, reading *The Sun* and occasionally lifting its right buttock to release a fart. Damn that useless bastard. Still, I'm partly to blame for its flabby, slothful condition, having spent years feeding it a diet of sweary cartoons, SAS memoirs and booze. I strain to think harder – or at least furrow my brow a bit harder, which pretty much amounts to the same thing these days. No, it's no use, I haven't got a clue what I'm doing right now or what I'm supposed to do next. Or even what it was I was doing just a few seconds ago. It's a bit like walking into a room and forgetting what you went in there for – but applied to your entire life.

I became a dad roughly twenty-two hours ago. But I think it may only have sunk into my consciousness during the four hours of sleep I managed overnight. Maybe it was spending a night alone in the house without my wife and the regimental sense of order she brings to things. Maybe it's the crushing weight of expectation and responsibility that fatherhood has suddenly placed on my delicate psyche. But something's malfunctioning up in my head and, no matter what special thinking face I pull, it's showing no signs of righting itself any time soon.

I feel like Sam Beckett in *Quantum Leap*. You know, where he suddenly woke up each week in a different person's body, unsure of where he was or what the hell was going on? But at least he had that bloke played by Dean Stockwell helping him to make sense of the situation with his little hand-held computer. Plus, he was invariably being chased by members of the Ku-Klux-Klan or taking part in a rodeo or engulfed in some other set of self-evident circumstances. Me? All I'm doing is standing in a nondescript residential street looking at my own wrist. I do this sometimes while loitering to make myself look less ridiculous to passers-by. Instead of looking at me and thinking, 'Look at that gormless imbecile standing around blinking into space like the fella out of *Quantum Leap*, only less handsome, brave and resourceful,' I imagine that they'll think: 'Wow, look at that dynamic and thrusting individual looking at his watch! He's the sort of guy for whom time is money and money is time! I wish I was as on the ball as him!' Unless they get close enough to realise that I'm not actually wearing a watch and am, in fact, just staring at my naked wrist.

Someone does come up the street. It's an old woman wearing a sleeveless jacket. I don't think it's the one I mistook for a gypsy confidence trickster, but it's so hard to tell. The only people who ever seem to wander past our house are elderly women in sleeveless jackets. Never a child in a duffel coat. Never a builder in a string vest. Never a coterie of topless young ladies wearing cycling helmets and running at top speed. Just elderly women, ambling slowly in sensible, sleeve-free outerwear.

At our old place loads of different people used to walk by. Once, I was skipping down the front steps en route to my weekly five-a-side match, all dressed up in my shorts and shin pads.

'Where are you playing, mate?' a nosey parker asked me as I made towards my Fiat Panda. When I turned round, guess who it was? Only Robbie Williams!

'Erm, just round the corner, under the flyover,' I said, trying to act all casual as if I didn't really know who he was.

'Need any spares?' he asked. He was with a couple of mates. I did a quick piece of mental arithmetic and realised that three extra players would unbalance the sides. I worried I'd look a bit of a prick in front of my mates if I turned our well-organised game of five versus five into a shambolic game of seven versus six just because I'd got star-struck by a former member of Take That. So I said: 'We've got even sides, I'm afraid.' Bear in mind, this wasn't recently. This was years back, when *Angels* had just come out and Williams was probably the most famous bloke in the country. It counted as a genuinely jaw-dropping celebrity encounter. But all I could say to him was, 'We've got even sides, I'm afraid.' Mind you, I think he respected me for it. Not that I require the respect of Robbie Williams to feel important or anything. He kind of grinned and shrugged at the strange nostalgic sensation that the word 'no' must have evoked. Then, probably just to emphasise the nature of the dynamic that prevails between celebrities and normals, he demanded that I give him and his mates a lift to the pub on my way to the game. Even though the pub was completely out of my way. Reader, I succumbed to that dynamic. They all crammed into my little Fiat and told me funny stories about their recently completed tour of Germany while I chauffeured them to their trendy gastro-boozer. And I ended up being ten minutes late for the game.

As I trotted on to the pitch and took up my position to defend a corner, one of my team-mates asked where I'd been.

'Just giving Robbie Williams a lift to the pub,' I replied. Unsure of how best to respond, he jabbed his knee firmly into the small of my back. And do you know what the strangest thing about that story is? It's not even a lie.

This old woman is staring at me funny. I don't think it's that she's spotted I'm not wearing a watch; it's a much more hostile stare than that realisation would demand. She's suspicious. I'm standing outside this rather twee, respectable little cottage with its tree in the front garden and flowers up the wall and what-have-you, and she's thinking something's not quite right. My face doesn't fit. I'm scruffy, I'm stupid-looking and I'm wearing shorts. And trainers. And a hooded top with two full-length sleeves. I can hardly blame her for thinking I'm a burglar really, can I?

'Can I help you?' she says all snootily, giving me the once-over.

Part of me enjoys this sort of situation. I like to confront people's prejudices and embrace the opportunity to ram them down their throats. I half-want this woman to just come out and accuse me of robbing so I can hit back with something cutting and witty like: 'What? You think just because I'm sporting sleeves and sports casuals that I can't be a property owner? That my snotty nose and dropped vowels have no place in your leafy hamlet? Well, I've got news for you! Have a little look at my driver's licence! That's right – this is my address! I'll show you the deeds if you want! Hard work bought me this. No hand-outs. No charity. Hard graft! Good, honest graft! Look at these hands! Feel them! Ravaged by hours of typing facetious nonsense for left-of-centre broadsheets, they are! Behold my worn larynx and dried-out tongue! Battered and bruised through years of broadcasting assignments for obscure digital TV channels, local radio stations and lamentable television advertising campaigns! That's right, madam, mine is the sooty, wind-battered face of the old-school working man who pulled himself up by the bootstraps! And I'll be damned if I'm to stand here on my own doorstep and be judged by the likes of you! I paid for every last brick of this house. Well, the bank helped. To be honest, I've got an interest-only mortgage that's stretching me pretty much to the limit. I mean, it'd probably make more sense to keep on renting, with prices what they are, but whaddaya gonna do? You've got to get your foot on the ladder sooner or later, ain't you?'

And maybe in the past that's exactly the sort of thing I would have said. Back when I was an angry young man with something to prove to the world. Before the wondrous epiphany of fatherhood showed me that the world is a harsh enough place already without the likes of me shouting the odds at every second person who gives them a funny look in the street. In other words, if this had happened to me about thirty-six hours ago, before I'd seen my first child born, endured a fitful night's sleep, gone home on my own, got all confused and emotional and wound up standing outside my house feeling vulnerable and in need of a reassuring cuddle.

'Erm, this is my house . . .' I tell the old woman.

'Yeessss,' she says slowly, suddenly switching her tone from one of suspicion to sympathy.

'But the thing is . . . my wife's just given birth.'

'What, in there?' she says pointing at the house.

'No, at the hospital . . .'

'Yeesssss . . .'

'And, well, I've got to go to the hospital now and bring her things. But I don't know what things, and I don't know how to get there, and I'm not sure what time visiting starts . . .'

She's already halfway up the alley by the time I've realised that I'm saying all this out loud.

'Well, good luck,' she says with a wave. 'I'm sure you'll be fine.'

Easy for her to say, the condescending old cow. Still, that little exchange did at least help jog my memory as to some of the matters in hand. I need to get back to the hospital, that much is clear. My wife and daughter need me. What for? Hard to say. Maybe I could change a nappy or read it a story or say something helpful to my missus about her emotions or her stitches or something. My role will become apparent with time, I'm sure. But how to get there? And when? And what was it that I was supposed to take with me? Something about a towel and some pants maybe. And some loose-fitting trousers? For the baby or the wife? Or me? Impossible to say. I shuffle up and down the garden path trying to decide what to do. This isn't like *Quantum Leap* at all. It's like *EastEnders* when Arthur Fowler nicked the Christmas Club money and went bananas on the allotment. I've got to get a grip.

The best thing to do in a situation like this is retrace one's steps. I remember the hours that followed the birth. I remember nipping outside the hospital to ring round the grandparents. As both sets of our parents are divorced, it was necessary for me to make four separate phone calls rather than two. One of the lesser-discussed side-effects of broken homes is the inflated phone bills incurred by the children in later years. My new daughter has four different grandparents all living separately from each other. This will make maintaining a relationship with each of them more difficult from a practical point of view. In an ideal world both couples would still be married and all living together in a tiny attic, like in *Charlie and The Chocolate Factory*. Even better, all of us – grandparents, parents, uncles, aunties and cousins – would live en masse in a gigantic shoe. That really would provide my little girl with the perfect support system in which to grow up. But modern society would doubtlessly label such a set-up as 'fanciful', 'outmoded' or 'a bit noncey'.

I call my mum first, knowing that she'll be the one who's fretting hardest. This is what I hear when she answers the phone:

'OHMYGOD CHRISTINHEAVEN! IKNEW SOMETHINGHADGONEWRONG! IJUSTFELTIT! AMOTHERKNOWS! IREMEMBER WHENIHAD YOURBROTHER HECAMEOUT WITHISCORD ROUNDHISNECK LIKEHEWAS BEING STRANGLED ANDOFCOURSE YOURFATHER WASN'TTHERE. *HE* WAS PROBABLYOFF ATONE OFHIS FUCKINGPARTIES! IWASSOSCARED ... ARRRRRRRGGGH ... sob ... sob ... Hello? Are you still there?'

'Yes.'

'Well, come on then, is it a boy or a girl?'

'It's a girl, and everyone's fine.'

'ARRRRRGHHHHH ... IKNEWIT! IKNEWIT WOULDBEAGIRL! AMOTHERKNOWS! I'MSO HAPPYNOBODYDIED! IHAVEN'TSTOPPED CRYING ALLMORNING ...'

I put the phone down and called my father-in-law. He too is the emotional sort. But then he's from Hungary, where being the emotional sort is the law.

'Oh, thank God!' he said shakily in his thick Hungarian accent. 'I am pleased about that.' Hungarians speak in very literal sentences, I've noticed.

'I'm sure,' I said, speaking quickly enough to suggest that I didn't have much time to talk. In fact, I was just trying to get off the phone before he started crying. But it was too late.

'I'm actually crying a bit right now', he said matter-of-factly, with a disconcerting tremble running through his central European twang.

'Oh, um ... well ... that's a shame,' I spluttered.

There's something about talking to foreigners that makes me come over all English.

'There's no shame in it,' he said soberly, sniffing up some rogue tears.

'No, of course, I just meant . . .'

'I cried when each of my own children was born. I cried when my parents died. I admit it to you without shame . . .'

'Crikey,' I thought to myself. 'He's off on the list of occasions on which he's cried. We could be here all day.'

'I cried in 1969, when I was still exiled from my homeland by the Communists and I received news via telegram from Budapest that . . .'

There are two things my father-in-law likes to do during everyday conversation. One is cite the precise year when a particular event took place. You might ask him if he fancies a cup of tea, and he will look into the middle distance, as if picturing a terrible battle or a majestic eagle in flight, and respond: '1957. That was the first time I was offered a cup of tea by an Englishman. . .' and then launch into a detailed anecdote surrounding the incident. Which I don't mind as long as I've got the time to listen. I mean it's a generally more lyrical and interesting way to respond than simply grumbling 'milk no sugar', like most English people do. The other thing he likes to chuck into everyday chatter is a nice bit of crying. I would say, in all the years I've known him, he's been crying about 20 per cent of the time. Not that I think he's any more miserable than the next bloke. In fact, once you get behind the strange accent and bouts of sobbing, you begin to realise that, relatively speaking, he's a pretty jolly fella. He's just not afraid to wear his heart on his sleeve. Johnny Hungarian is like that. Probably something to do with all those years of war and trauma, the Commies, the Nazis, all that other stuff.

What other stuff? I don't know. I suppose I should know having been involved with this Hungarian family for the past twelve years, but I've never been that attentive when it comes to listening to family history. Whenever dinnertime conversation turns to Hungary's long history of persecution, war and injustice (if, indeed, that is what's been going on over there throughout history – as I say, I have no way of knowing), I just sort of drift off into my own, imagined idea of Hungary. My imaginary Hungary features moustachioed men in colourful, billowing trousers, jaunty waistcoats and curly shoes who fight with giant sabres atop magical flying carpets while dusky ladies dressed in silks perform sexy dance routines with snakes wrapped around them. And yes, I am aware that my imaginary Hungary is not only misinformed and a bit racist but probably based more closely on Turkish stereotypes than Hungarian ones. But what are Hungarian stereotypes? There are none! And for that they've only got themselves to blame. What do you think of when you think of Hungary? Shut your eyes and think of it right now. See? Nothing! Now perhaps you can appreciate my attitude towards the whole place. I mean, I've been to Hungary a few times, and I still can't think of much I'd associate with the place. Other than my father-in-law. And men crying.

'I cried a bit myself,' I told him, partly to distract him from crying and partly because I wanted him to know that I too have some semblance of human emotion hidden somewhere deep beneath my galvanised exterior of trite cynicism, muddled irony, English reserve and juvenile half-wittery.

'What? You? Really?' he said.

'Yes, 'fraid so. Couldn't help myself,' I said proudly.

There was a silence. I chose to interpret the silence as happiness. Perhaps a bit of pride. And maybe a bit of relief that his son-in-law was not necessarily the immature berk he'd taken him for over the past twelve years.

'Well done,' he said, his endorsement filling me with pride.

'I suppose I could do with being just a tiny bit more Hungarian myself in certain ways,' I thought to myself. 'Show some emotion once in a while. Take things more seriously. Begin each anecdote with an announcement of the year in which it took place. One thing is for sure – I'll definitely be investing in a jaunty waistcoat.'

Next I had to call my mother-in-law, then my dad. I figured they could wait a bit longer to get the good news on account of them being so unemotional. They care not for the flim-flam and frippery of emotional jabber and sentimental discourse. They deal in hard facts and rigour. I called them last, because I knew they would be less concerned about anything going wrong during the birth. It's not that they don't care. Their brains are just too relentlessly rational to let them worry about much. Both of them are a bit like Rain Man, I suppose. Give them cold hard information, and they're as good as gold. Start trying to engage them in the stuff of human heartache and they'll start bashing themselves about the head and shouting, 'Qantas never crashed!' or something.

With this in mind, I took care to deliver the good news to my mother-in-law in a cold, flat monotone – as if I were working on a checkout at Tesco and requesting a price check on six-packs of Club biscuits. I wasn't about to insult the woman by dressing the news up in needless ceremony or frivolous hoop-la: I've got more respect for her than that. She responded with the words 'I thought so', which made me feel ever so slightly stupid for even bothering to give her the news. Of course you've had the baby! Isn't it obvious? Don't you know that all statistics on childbirth over the past ten years among women of a similar age, weight and socio-economic background pointed towards this precise outcome, you blithering idiot?! Well, anyway, that's my mother-in-law for you. Steely and stern. Like Clint Eastwood but with a computer for a brain and a predilection for pottery. I knew she was feeling mushy and gleeful on the inside, she just wouldn't let me see it. As a son-in-law, I am a disappointment to her. But if she's Clint, then I hope she at least sees me as that orang-utan he starred alongside in *Any Which Way But Loose*.

Finally I contacted my dad. 'Sorry to bother you, I just didn't want you to worry,' I say, immediately realising I'd chosen the wrong tack.

'Why would I be worrying?' he demanded.

'Erm, I dunno, I didn't mean worry. I meant "wonder". I didn't want you to wonder what might be happening with the baby and all that.'

'In what sense?' he persisted sternly.

'Ey?'

'In what sense didn't you want me to wonder about the baby *and all that?*'

'Er, well, you know, I thought you might be sat at home thinking something like "I wonder if that baby has been born yet".'

'No. I wasn't thinking that. I knew perfectly well that you would call once the baby had been born, so what would be the point of wondering about it in the meantime?'

Remember Mr Logic out of *Viz*? That's what my dad acts like sometimes.

'Yes. Quite right,' I venture with a gulp. 'Well, you were right. The baby was born and I have called you. Just as you envisaged.'

'I know.'

'I know you know.'

'Good. Well. Congratulations.'

'Thanks.'

Luckily for both him and me, I know full well that my dad is a big, cuddly pussycat inside. The trick is to not let him know that you know he's a big, cuddly pussycat. If you do, he will only overcompensate by starting to act like Mr Spock. I can ignore it because I have seen his softer side on countless unguarded occasions.

One of my favourites was on a cold winter's afternoon in Brighton about twelve years ago. It was the first time he had met my girlfriend and future wife. 'He's a bit gruff at first but just a big cuddly pussycat inside,' I'd warned her, hoping to Christ that he did something pussycat-ish at some stage to back up my claims. He didn't let me down. After a lunch throughout which he'd been mildly gruff, we were walking along the busy high street when our attentions turned to a distressed young lady screaming at the top of her voice at no one in particular, 'HELP ME! HELP ME! I CAN'T TAKE THIS! I'M SO SAD!' Possibly the only way of describing her would be as a crack whore. Mangled teeth, grubby hair, skeletal features, and bulgy, psychotic eyes. You know the type. This being a cold winter's afternoon on an English high street, it goes without saying that nobody stopped to help her. Why would they? She was probably just shouting at an imaginary voice in her head that taunted her with persistent renditions of Brotherhood of Man's back catalogue whenever the drug supplies ran low in her veins. Fearing that any sort of encounter with her might ruin my delicately balanced afternoon, I quickened my step. Then, suddenly, I noticed my old man walking towards her.

'Dad! What the fuck are you doing?!' I squealed like a big, soppy girl. But it was too late. He already had a comforting arm around the crack whore's shoulder.

'What's the matter?' he asked gently.

'Oh Christ!' I muttered under my breath in sulky, adolescent despair. The crack whore began to explain her predicament to him. I can't remember the exact details, but it was something to do with an absentee boyfriend, an unscrupulous landlord and a dealer who steadfastly refused to entertain the notion of credit. She actually made it sound quite convincing and poignant. As soon as my dad started talking to her, she stopped screaming like a mentalist and just sobbed gently. I stood there with my mouth open, my idiotic brain convincing itself that my girlfriend would probably call off our relationship on the basis of my dad being a crack whore botherer.

'I'm really sorry about this,' I told her.

'Why? I think it's really nice. No one else bothered to help her,' she replied, which made me feel a bit stupid for apologising.

My dad talked for about twenty minutes with the crack whore, asking her about the specifics of her problems, offering nuggets of sympathy and pearls of advice. God knows what he knew about the tribulations of being a crack whore, but he looked as if he was doing his best to understand. Throughout the conversation he kept a comforting arm wrapped around her, unconcerned by the visible muck that caked her entire person. She seemed so touched and appreciative. My girlfriend looked awestruck by his compassion. I just stood there feeling like a flimsy, unsympathetic drip for reacting in the way I had. Eventually he gave her some money to get herself a room for the night. That was probably the bit that resonated most strongly in my mind. The lessons I should have learned from my father that day were: have the courage to help other people, however alien and intimidating they may appear; show some humanity and try to empathise with those less fortunate than yourself; listen to their problems, understand their plight and lend a helping hand wherever you can. But the only lesson I chose to learn was: 'If someone's crying, give them twenty quid. That'll shut them up.'

Unfortunately I have relied on cash hand-outs as a substitute for genuine compassion ever since. Made your niece cry in an over-exuberant play fight? Bung her a tenner. Uncle weeping over recently deceased aunt? That'd probably take more like fifty or sixty quid. You can imagine how much I've spent on my father-in-law over the years.

Of course my dad has taught me loads of other valuable lessons over the years, too. But I can't say I've always been a receptive pupil. He tried to teach me chess once, but it never worked out. I only saw him on the odd Saturday, so I'd always forget what he'd already taught me in between lessons. Plus, on that particular day of the week I always had half a mind on what time *Dukes of Hazzard* was starting. I mean, how the fuck could I have maintained interest in him going on about castling when the Dukes were gearing up to make a mockery once again of Boss Hogg's ludicrous brand of redneck law enforcement?

Right, so where was I? Oh yeah, I rang round the grandparents, went back to the hospital and hung around in a woozy, faintly surreal state of family bliss. The baby, much tinier than I could possibly have imagined it would be, lay there sleeping. My wife and I gazed wordlessly at each other, trying to absorb everything that had happened and what the rest of our lives were going to be about. We also shared a large bag of Mini Cheddars. When the baby woke up, my wife fed her and then I tried to change her nappy. It was terrifying: her tiny limbs seemed so delicate and fragile that I dithered as hesitantly as an ill-qualified bomb-disposal expert. She cried throughout the whole distressing experience, and in the end a nurse had to come over and help. I felt inadequate and a bit sad. Then it was time to leave.

But before I left, my wife gave me a list. Yes! That's it, the precious list! She scrawled it on a napkin with her shaky hand, which was still covered in dressing and bits of tube. In a tiny red bookie's biro that I found in my pocket. And now I'm standing on my garden path, patting all of my pockets to check if the list is hiding in one of them. I go back into the house. I spend a few pointless moments opening drawers full of junk and phone bills and bank statements, throwing them around and making a strange frustrated growl. I run up and down the stairs a few times, opening doors, scanning rooms for the list.

I left that hospital with so much information. Important, precious information. Information that my brain immediately flushed out the moment I walked out through the doors. Perhaps I'm being harsh on my brain: perhaps it's not lazy, just full: full with all the earth-shattering events of yesterday; all the concerns and fears about the future; all those images of my wife and daughter lying in the hospital bed together; so many thoughts, ideas, colours, shapes, smells and things. Damned, relentless things. Ordinarily my brain has about a dozen or so things to compute on an average day. Suddenly it's being overloaded to a million times its usual capacity. It's close to collapse. Trying to recall the details of what I'm supposed to be doing this morning could be the wafer-thin mint that finally causes it to explode and dribble out of my nostrils in liquid form.

If only I could find this list. The list will tell me what I need to bring to the hospital. The list will tell me what time visiting hours start. The list will tell me how to get there, where to park, what to say to my wife and how to change the baby's nappy without more humiliating interventions by the nurses. The list will probably even come with handy illustrations. Yes, the precious, precious list will make everything all right.

Only the list isn't here. Deep down, I think I always knew it wasn't here. Even before I lost my temper with myself and started turning over the mattress on our bed, pulling open kitchen drawers and turning waste paper baskets upside down. Where did it go? Discarded on my way out of the maternity ward? Dropped on the floor of my brother's car when he gave me a lift home from the hozzy last night? Accidentally eaten in my sleep? Who knows? It's probably just gone the same way as all the other lists, receipts, airline tickets and sundry important bits of paper I've lost over the years. Consigned to the vast dustbin of forgetfulness, disorganisation and inefficiency that has hindered my everyday life since childhood. Oh, it may seem funny and charming and quirky when you're twelve or twenty or even thirty-one. When the worst thing that can happen is that you forget to switch off your own gas oven and accidentally kill yourself and the cat. But I am now responsible for another human being. I have to get sane. I need to whip my brain into shape and start making sense of what the hell it is I'm supposed to be doing. It's no longer enough to flick on my mental lights once or twice a day. They need to be on constantly: I must be focused, diligent and sharp at all times. Like a sniper, or the bloke who does my book-keeping.

I make a mental note to lose fewer notes. Then I grab a giant hold-all, fill it with half the contents of my wife's wardrobe, chuck in a couple of towels and some wet wipes for good measure and call a cab to take me to the hospital.

12
TUPPERWEAR

That sound. Why won't it stop? It's been going on for ages. What is it? It can't be crying. I'm pretty sure it's not screaming either. Those sounds are like old friends to me now, I'd recognise them anywhere. This is different. Is someone talking to me again? I wish people would stop doing that. Can't they see I'm tired? Their words are only making things worse.

But hang on, I don't think it's words I can hear. It's something else, something just as familiar but twice as irritating. It's a knock at the door. Again. I snarl and hunch my shoulders like a wildcat primed for attack. Only I am woozy and tired and feel a bit sick – like one of those lions in the zoo which has just been shot in the arse with a tranquilliser dart after trying to savage a tourist. I am dressed in some nylon football shorts and a vest. I am unshaven. The last time I looked at my face in the mirror (something I'm generally trying to avoid), I looked about eighty years old. Suffice to say, I'm not really in the mood to receive visitors right now. But what can I do? They just keep coming. I used to pride myself on keeping the borders of my home tightly secured against unwanted guests, but what can I tell you? I'm just too dazed and disorientated to resist. One week into fatherhood, and I've already surrendered at least 50 per cent of the principles I've always held dear.

I open the door and in they traipse. No 'Hello's, no 'How you doing?'s. No 'Hey, you look great in those shorts!' They just push past me and start looking for the baby. This must have been what Joseph felt like when all the wise men and shepherds starting tipping up at the stable door that night. But at least that lot brought precious gifts. All I've got is a gaggle of grim-faced Hungarians carrying Tupperware boxes filled with a brown substance that I'm assuming passes for one of their national dishes.

'Where is she?' one of them asks as they pass through the front room.

'She's asleep upstairs,' I say, trying to conjure some merriment in my voice.

They silently trundle upstairs and surround the cot. I just hope they don't wake her up. I mean, imagine coming round from a nice kip to be confronted by three strange Hungarians wearing unruly beards, maroon polo necks and stony, expressionless faces. Thank God, her eyes aren't working properly yet or she might be emotionally scarred for life.

I leave them to it. It's pointless to resist. It's best just to smile, stick the kettle on and try to take advantage of the fact that someone else is keeping an eye on the baby by sneaking off to the toilet for a fifteen-minute kip on the floor.

It's only been a week, and I'm already obsessing over where my next nap is coming from. I tell my wife I'm going to make her a sandwich so I can sleep for five minutes while leaning against the fridge. I nipped out to the shops for some milk and stole twenty minutes on a park bench. I am trying to master the art of sleeping with my eyes open, so nobody will be able to tell. Failing that, I may just draw eyeballs on to my eyelids.

I know what you're thinking: how tired can you possibly get in just one week? Well, you have to understand that, until very recently, I was used to a great deal of sleep. I ordinarily liked to get ten hours, even on a school night. The constant interruptions I've had to my deep, peaceful slumbers over the past seven days are more than my body can handle. Basically, I've spoiled myself. That's one of the problems with having your first child in your thirties. By that stage you're already a bit set in your ways: you've spent too many years becoming accustomed to a self-indulgent lifestyle. I mean, my parents started having kids when they were in their early twenties, when they hadn't yet had a chance to cultivate a lifestyle defined by lazy TV marathons, binge-drinking and expensive convenience food from the Sainsbury's Taste The Difference range (or whatever the luxury equivalents were in their day: Radio Luxembourg and a beef-dripping sandwich, I suppose). They had no idea that there was any sort of life beyond sleep deprivation, shit and tears. They had no problem with it. As George Michael once so rightly pointed out: ignorance is kind to the heart and mind. I think he was talking about someone having it off with a floozy behind their girlfriend's back, but, like so many of his songs (with the possible exception of 'Wake Me Up Before You Go Go'), the sentiment was universally applicable.

But of course, none of this is really surprising. I knew I'd be tired. One of the appeals of fatherhood was that it would force me to be a less lazy person. If I come out of the next few months feeling like a Maggie Thatcher-type automaton who only requires four hours of sleep per day in order to function properly, then it'll all have been worthwhile.

The non-stop merry-go-round of visitors doesn't make things any less confusing. An aunt leaves as an old schoolfriend arrives. They disappear, to be replaced by a second cousin. She sticks around for three hours and only pushes off once two of your wife's former colleagues show up. Next thing you know, some mate of a mate who you're almost certain you've never actually met before but who works nearby has appeared on the doorstep clutching a bunch of tatty-looking tulips and wondering if it'd be all right if she came in and just stared at the baby for half an hour. The weirdo. I don't mean to sound cruel, but I'm struggling to see what the attraction is anyway. Obviously, to my eyes the baby's great. But she's my baby. I can stare at her for ages and not get bored. When I say 'ages', I mean about thirty minutes. She doesn't actually do much in the way of comic turns or diverting conversation, so half an hour is pretty much my limit. Still, that's a good fifteen minutes more than I'm usually able to concentrate on anything else without getting distracted and checking to see if there's anything good on telly.

How do they even know about the baby? I blame Facebook. I knew I shouldn't have uploaded all those pictures when I got in from the hospital on the day of the birth. I wasn't thinking straight. It didn't really dawn on me how inappropriate the pictures were for public consumption until my wife got home and saw what I'd done.

'What the fuck?!' was all she was able to say once she'd logged on. Nothing says 'Home Sweet Home' quite like your missus breastfeeding the baby while fiddling about on Facebook with her spare hand.

'Oh, yeah,' I said, glancing over her shoulder at the pictures. 'I put them up the other night – I thought people would like to see.'

I'd called the album 'Our New Arrival'. As she clicked through the images, it was like her mouth was struggling to keep up with her brain. She just kept saying, 'What . . . the . . . fuck?' like a mantra.

One of the baby all covered in goo. One of me holding her in my cool surgical scrubs. One of my wife covered in sweat and blood and looking as if a little part of her soul had just died. Another of her splayed out on the bed in exhaustion with her boobies showing. I'd thought they were the very epitome of heart-warming family snaps when I uploaded them. I wanted all those friends, relatives, obscure work colleagues from yesteryear and completely random strangers who had befriended me on Facebook to share in my joy. But, on reflection, I maybe should have been a bit more selective about how much joy I shared. I mean, I think my wife is the most gorgeous woman in the world. But I'll be honest, she didn't look her best in those pictures. Who does look their best forty minutes after boshing a seven-and-a-half-pound human being out of their arse? I could have at least left the topless pics out, I suppose.

'What were you thinking?' she eventually asked, once she'd stopped spluttering in astonishment.

'Come on, it's not like they're all porny or anything, is

it?' I pleaded. 'These are your breasts in their most natural state. No one would look at them in a pervy way, if that's what you're thinking.'

'No, that's not what I'm thinking,' she said.

Which was weird. Because as I said the words I was secretly thinking about how I might react if one of my Facebook friends had posted a similar picture of their wife. In all honesty, I don't think I would have thought that it was natural and touching and motherly. I think I would have thought something like: 'Wow-wee, it's my mate's wife's boobies! Yeee-ha! I never thought I'd get a butcher's at those! I think I'll download them to my hard disk immediately for future reference.' Still, she's not to know that.

'It's not about people perving over them,' she reiterated.

'What's it about then?' I asked.

'It's about . . . just not wanting people to see them at all.'

'Exactly, in case they perv over them.'

'No. I just don't exactly look at my best, do I?'

'I think naked breasts are naked breasts,' I said, not quite sure where I was going. 'I mean, they don't have to be covered in baby oil or have tassels on them to look nice.'

'You're a fucking dick, d'you know that?' she said calmly. 'Think of it this way: would you want me to take a picture of you just after an operation with your knob dangling about and post it on the internet?'

'Depends,' I mused. 'Would the operation have actually been on my knob? Because I remember I had an operation on my balls once, and they turned all the colours of the rainbow.'

She didn't answer.

'Anyway, it's a moot point,' I said, somewhat boldly considering I wasn't quite sure what 'moot point' actually meant. 'They didn't operate on your boobs. They didn't even touch your boobs, did they? Or did they?'

There was a silence. She clicked on the final picture. It was an uncompromising close-up of her right breast with our daughter blindly trying to locate the nipple with her mouth. She looked up from the screen and glared at me awaiting explanation.

'You look like a, what d'you call it, an earth mother?' I smiled reassuringly.

'A what?'

'You know, like one of them African women out of the documentaries with the dangling boobs and the plates in their mouths.'

'You're not making this any better,' she explained.

I deleted the pictures. Later I decided to shut down my Facebook account altogether to avoid similar mishaps. But by that stage it was too late. The word was out, and well-wishers were already banging at the door like the zombies from *Night of the Living Dead*. Before the Hungarians have even left, one of the neighbours knocks round with a bottle of red wine. She's the posh sort you get round here: no sleeves, plenty of pearls and a dead nice cut-glass accent.

'It's not for the baby,' she quips as she hands me the booze, 'but I thought you might be in need of a glass or two this evening once you've got her off to sleep . . . oh, I see, you're opening it now. Well, fair enough, I suppose.'

Judging by her reaction, I'm guessing it's still early.

How am I supposed to know? My existence is no longer fashioned around the narrow-minded conventions of twenty-four-hour time-keeping. I answer not to Greenwich Mean Time but to the whimsical sleeping patterns of a tiny baby. This being the height of summer, there's almost constant daylight, which makes it even easier to lose sight of what time it is in the real world. I learned days ago that looking at clocks only crushes your will to carry on. So you ignore time, you sleep when you can and drink whenever circumstances allow. That's why I am currently in the kitchen pouring myself a tumblerful of this plonk. I knock it back in two healthy gulps. There, that's better. I've never really been a daytime drinker, but right now it feels like all the usual rules of decency have been temporarily suspended. It's like you imagine it might be after a nuclear attack on London: the survivors could just race down to the nearest PC World and nick whatever they like, then have sex with a stranger on the way home. I mean, who'd be asking questions, right?

As I use my arm to wipe the red wine from my mouth, the neighbour eyes me with pity and a tiny bit of fear.

'Sorry,' I say. 'My manners! D'you want a bit?'

Rather than pour her a fresh glass, I find myself just offering her the dregs of what's left in mine. She politely declines and asks to see the baby. I direct her upstairs to join the Hungarians. Then I reload my tumbler.

I catch sight of my reflection in the kitchen window. It's not pretty. The gradual hair loss I've been experiencing over the past five years seems to have accelerated in recent days. It's thinner than ever on top. Combined with my vest-and-shorts get-up, I look like I'm going to a fancy dress party as a badly out-of-shape Steve Ovett. I thought fatherhood would make me look more respectable. Turn me into the sort of bloke who shaves every morning, stands upright at all times and wears a tie even when he hasn't got a meeting that day. But instead I am the sort of bloke who stands in his kitchen at 11 a.m. in a vest slurping mid-priced Shiraz and wondering if any of his visitors would think it was weird if he crawled under the table for a fifteen-minute snooze.

Before I get a chance to do so, they've all come back downstairs.

'Is she still sleeping?' I ask.

'No, of course not,' says my father-in-law. 'She's crying. Can't you hear her?'

I concentrate for a few seconds, willing my brain to register what my ears are telling it. Yep, I suppose he might be right – that does sound like a baby crying.

'Oh yeah, sorry, I though that was the bathroom fan,' I mutter, then shuffle upstairs to comfort the baby. By 'comfort' I mean get her out of her cot and hand her to my wife for a feed. I discover my wife sprawled out in the bedroom with her legs in the bed but her hands and face on the floor. She must have been so tired that she fell asleep before she could actually manage to get herself into position. We've both been doing a bit of that lately. I suddenly lost consciousness while trying to fit a Scart lead into the back of the telly the other day. She found me on one knee with my eyes shut and a long stream of dribble protruding from my lower lip. Right now she looks like one of those fossilised victims of ancient volcano eruptions who were encased in molten lava while in the middle of an everyday chore. I prod her shoulder with my foot. She doesn't move.

'Shit . . . are you . . . are you dead?' I mumble. My foggy, delirious brain finds it difficult to panic in the way you might have thought it would. I just think: 'How will we stop the baby crying if she's dead? We won't be able to feed it. I'll have to get one of the Hungarians to nip out for some SMA.'

Suddenly her eyes blink open, and she assumes a more conventional position. I hand her the crying child, and we exchange a wordless glance of baggy-eyed bewilderment as she fastens it to her breast. This is pretty much how we've been communicating for days now. This is a war, and we are soldiers on the front line. We just have to get through it as best we can; no words could possibly make things any easier. Verbal communication just seems like pointless and indulgent showmanship now, mere noise used to dress up crude human experience as something more poetic than it actually is. Our challenges are self-evident: keep the baby warm, happy and fed, and try to sleep whenever and wherever we can. It's a case of just switching off and letting The Force guide us from there.

Downstairs the Hungarians are getting on well with the posh neighbour. They're all saying things like 'Doesn't she look like her mother?' and 'Yes, but I also think there's a hint of her father'. I've noticed everyone's been saying this sort of stuff over the past few days. It's like a default language that people automatically slip into when they are in the presence of a new-born baby. I play along, chipping in with remarks like 'Yes, she has the same shaped jaw-line as my mother, but she definitely has Uncle Tom's ears!'.

Everyone nods. But, as they gaze upon her in her cot, I suspect their thoughts are just as prosaic as my own: 'Yep, that's a baby all right. Isn't it small? Not doing much, is it? Better think of something to say. Maybe I'll say it looks a bit like its mother.'

Most of the thoughts that float through your brain when you're looking at a baby are meaningless. They're not really even thoughts at all, more like strange, formless reactions you feel in the gut and the heart. What do they call them again? That's it: 'emotions'. Staring at a baby is a hypnotic experience that most of us seem to find soothing and curiously uplifting. But some people claim to derive insight from staring at this fledgling being as it lies there doing sod all. They say things like 'She's going to be a joker, this one', while nodding their head knowingly. Or 'She's got such intelligent eyes', even though her eyes are almost permanently shut. Which, if you want to be pedantic about it, is almost the opposite of intelligent eyes. Shut eyes are stupid eyes. But all of that's neither here nor there really, because the people saying this stuff are just saying it to pass the time while they sip tea and eat biscuits and prepare to have one last look at the baby before naffing off.

'Would you like more tea, anyone?' I ask the Anglo-Hungarian throng.

Everyone shakes their head, because they still haven't finished the cups I gave them five minutes ago. 'How about more biscuits?' More head-shakes. 'Oh well,' I say, 'the baby will have finished feeding in about ten minutes. I'll bring her down so you can have another stare before you go.'

Everyone seems to perk up when I say this, and they start to chatter among themselves again.

'Of course, it's perfectly clear that she is going to be extremely artistic,' I hear someone say as I wander into the kitchen looking for something to eat.

I may sound a bit moany and resentful toward these house guests, but they're not all bad. These Hungarians are not the first people to have turned up bearing Tupperware boxes containing home-cooked meals. People also bring flowers, fruit and magazines. My mum even brought some Berocca soluble vitamins the other day. We are being treated like invalids who are slowly dying. Frankly, I could get used to it. I pour the brown Hungarian matter into a pan, let it simmer for five minutes, then spread some between two pieces of Hovis with some ketchup. I feel instantly energised.

'Does anyone want any of this . . . stuff?' I say, lumbering back into the front room with a mouthful of sandwich. But the neighbour has gone, and the remaining Hungarians are busily saying goodbye to my wife. One of them is claiming that the baby has a 'wise face' and 'unusually dexterous hands'.

'Bye then!' I cheer, firing crumbs across the hallway as they make towards the exit. I don't know whether it's the breakfast wine or the Hungarian sandwich or the fact that the house is about to be guest-free for the first time in days, but I am overwhelmed with a fleeting sense of euphoria. The door shuts, and I look at my wife and daughter. Unusually, none of us are sleeping or crying. I sigh a contented sigh. Here we are, cocooned in a fuzzy-headed little netherworld where days are spelt out by cups of tea, slices of cake, nappy changes, naps and unsolicited visitors. I may not have shaved, worked or exercised in days. I may feel entirely cut off from the real, civilised world that is presumably still turning outside the front door. I may be wearing a vest and feeling so tired I could puke. But I like it. It feels strangely blissful. I'm just not quite sure you could call this living.

13
POKER

I am lying on my bed trapped somewhere between asleep and awake, with the baby splayed out on my chest. I have dribbled all over her head. We are both snapped back to consciousness by the sound of someone complaining about the inadequacy of local parking facilities.

'Your granddad's here,' I tell the baby, gently wiping some of my drool from her hair.

Gently I pick her up and softly pad downstairs with her cradled in my arms. I emerge into the living room brandishing her at my dad. He frowns at me.

'Oh my God! What are you holding her like that for?' he says. I look down at the baby who looks quite happy. But what do I know?

'Give her to me,' he says, holding out his arms and shaking his head wearily. 'The poor little thing will get crippled lying there like that.'

My brain is tired and disorientated enough to take his word for it. In the SAS they weaken prisoners' minds for interrogation by keeping them awake for days on end, stood on one leg in a cold room with the crackle of an untuned radio pumped loudly into their ears – which doesn't sound a million miles away from the circumstances

I've been living under for the past couple of weeks. So if my dad tells me I'm holding the baby wrong, then I'm in no fit state to disagree. Right now he could tell me that there was no baby at all and that I'd actually been cradling a large bag of brown sugar with a baby's face Sellotaped to it for the past few hours. I'd just smile, nod, squish the baby into the kitchen cupboard above the kettle and curl up on the sofa for a nice kip.

'Jesus, careful! You nearly dropped her!' he shrieks as I hand her to him.

I smile apologetically.

'Did I?' I say, looking around the room for confirmation. But the only other person there is my wife, who is so tired that she's starting to look like that snake out of *The Jungle Book* with the weird, spinning eyes. I won't get any sense out of her.

'Yes, I think I did nearly drop her,' I say to my dad with a slight, inexplicable giggle in my voice. 'Sorry.'

He holds her in his arms and talks soothingly to her. 'What are we going to do about your stupid daddy?' he says. 'We'll have to report him to social services, won't we? It's not safe for you here. He's an idiot.'

I stand beside them, listening, nodding and slouching in a gormless sort of a way. He may be slagging me off, but he's doing it in a special baby voice that I actually find quite comforting. Anyway, what do I care if he thinks I'm an incompetent idiot? It's better than him thinking I'm in total control – then he'd never offer to help. Maybe if I actually had dropped the baby when I was coming down the stairs, he might have agreed to take her off our hands for a night or two while we caught up on some sleep and got our heads together.

'What's this they've got you dressed in?' he says, regarding the West Ham pyjamas I bought her with abject disgust. 'How revolting! You poor thing – being dressed up like a clown in this tasteless crap.' I just grin and nod some more.

When my dad was in his early twenties, he ran a rock 'n' roll club with his brothers called The Big Beat. It was in Harrow, north London, and they managed to attract some of the top bands of the time: The Animals, The Yardbirds, The Moody Blues – even The High Numbers, who went on to become The Who. Pretty cool, huh?

Kids would come from all over London to watch bands at The Big Beat. Sometimes different gangs would end up fighting on the dance floor, so my dad hired a couple of meatheads to keep the peace. Trouble was, they had such an uncompromising approach to their work that they ended up causing more aggro than the clientele themselves. Once they chased a gang of bike-chain-wielding hoodlums out of the club and all the way down the street outside. After twenty minutes they still hadn't come back, and my dad started to worry that they might have been nicked or something. Eventually one of the meatheads reappeared over the horizon, puffing, wheezing and chuckling all at once.

'What happened?' asked my dad.

'Well, I managed to catch up with one lad outside the train station,' panted the goon.

'And?' said Dad.

'And I whacked him over the head with me cosh. Laid him spark out!'

'So what's the joke?' Dad enquired.

'The joke was, he weren't one of the kids we'd been chasing. Everyone got muddled up in the crowds. Turns out he was just some poor bastard running for a train!'

I like it when my dad tells me stories about The Big Beat. Then again, I like it when anyone tells me lightly comedic tales of calamitous street violence. But the stories surrounding that club have particular relevance in my mind because it's where my parents met.

When my mum was sixteen, she dreamed of hanging out at The Big Beat. It may have been housed in the sleepy, civic environs of the Harrow Weald Memorial Hall, but it was still the hottest spot for miles around. Problem was, she was too young. Then she got pally with a girl called Michelle Delaney, who said she could get her in no problem, because her brothers ran the place. So one Friday night my mum put on her best clobber, did her hair up in a gigantic beehive and snuck out of the house behind her parents' back. True to her word, Michelle managed to get both of them past the burly doormen with ease.

It was while she was waiting to check her coat in at the cloakroom that she first clocked my dad, standing there in his fancy suit with a fag on the go. As their eyes met, she reckons it was one of those spine-tingling romantic moments. You know, like there was some sort of instant magnetism between them. It sounds corny, I suppose, but I like to suspend my cynicism whenever she recounts the story. After all, that was the precise moment that I came into being, in some kind of faraway, notional sense at least. It's better than your mum telling you that your dad got hold of her at the work's Christmas do after failing to cop off with her better-looking mate.

They then fell in love and started courting. My mum's parents, who were a bit prim and aspirational, didn't approve. They probably dreamed of mum one day marrying a dreary accountant from a slightly better-off family who would eventually buy her a semi-detached house in Hertfordshire and condemn her to a life of domesticity and Valium abuse. They certainly didn't envisage her taking up with a wannabe rock 'n' roll impresario who lived on the estate up the road.

My dad's family was huge. They all lived together on a council estate in Stanmore. His Irish father and Scouse mum churned out kids at the prolific rate that only Roman Catholics can muster. I suppose it was something to do with the inherently lairy mix of Irish, Scouse and London cultures that may have lent my dad, the oldest of eight kids, a certain cocksure swagger.

If there was one thing my mum's mum didn't like, it was cocksure swagger. She objected to anyone with even the faintest whiff of self-confidence about them. She thought people like that were show-offs. My dad would turn up at their little home in Harrow in his old man's car, wearing his flashy clothes, talking his flashy talk and having the audacity to look my grandma in the eye when he spoke to her. The flaming cheek of the man! She generally preferred people to be painfully inhibited. She saw a certain sort of warped dignity in it, I suppose. Suffice to say, my dad was her living, breathing nightmare. He epitomised a post-war generation that wanted more out of life than retarded, buttoned-down conformity. They wanted to be treated as equals! They wanted to wear nice clothes and drive fast cars just like the posh kids! They wanted to dance to loud rock 'n' roll music and cast off the suffocating social conventions of yesteryear! And most of all they wanted to get your sixteen-year-old daughter pregnant! Well, maybe that last bit wasn't an explicit part of my dad's manifesto, but it was nevertheless what he did.

Mum's parents weren't the sorts to come over all Claire Rayner in that sort of situation. There was no 'Never mind, luv, let's all sit down and talk about what we should do'. It was more a case of 'Your father and I have decided that you'll have the baby in secret, then give it up for adoption to the nuns'. What was my mum supposed to do? Or my dad, for that matter? I mean, he'd got a girl five years his junior up the spout. They'd only been going out six months. He was lucky my granddad didn't come round the estate with a shotgun.

So off they sent her to some grim hospital, where she gave birth to a baby daughter in the most unspeakably painful and heartbreaking circumstances. She named it Caroline. My dad was forbidden from seeing them, but he managed to creep in behind everyone's back and briefly meet his little daughter soon after she was born. A few days later she was taken away from my poor mum, who, of course, never really got over it. The laws back then stopped her from trying to contact Caroline directly, but over the years she wrote tons of letters to her and sent them to the adoption society. The adoption society weren't allowed to notify Caroline of the letters, but Mum hoped she might one day get curious and come looking for them. And years later Caroline did get in touch. Only she was no longer

Caroline. She had grown up, with the help of a little operation, to be none other than the actor Ross Kemp!

No, not really. Would have been a nice twist though, wouldn't it?

So, just to be clear: everything so far is true other than the bit about Ross Kemp being my long-lost sister. Got it? Good. Right, anyway, in spite of all this messy business, Mum and Dad eventually got together. When mum's parents found out that she was still knocking about with dad, they went ballistic and threw her out of the house.

They finally got married in 1964, when she was twenty and he was twenty-five. They had my three brothers within the first three years of their marriage. They lived in a succession of council houses for the next ten years or so, my dad scraping together a few quid however he could, first as a road manager for rock bands like The Searchers and later as a film extra. In the early 1970s he went all radical and got involved in the Workers' Revolutionary Party. During the three-day week, when civil unrest simmered and tanks took to the streets of London, the government even bugged my parents' phone. But I don't think he was really ready to blow anyone up or commandeer the apparatus of the state. He was basically a hippy who'd read too many books. While he banged on about Trotsky and social injustice and how all property was theft, Mum would just smile, nod, carry on doing the dishes and wonder how they were going to pay the gas bill. Then in 1975 they had me – the youngest by seven years. And about three years after that they split up. My dad got a proper job, remarried and a few years later had my younger sister with his new wife.

One day, when I was nineteen, Mum told me to come

into the living room and sit down because she had something to tell me. Her unusually formal, melodramatic tone made me come over all queasy. It didn't help that I had been smoking skunk weed all afternoon in my bedroom and she had managed to catch me just as I'd briefly crept out in search of a sandwich. As my head started to swim with nausea, she suddenly burst out crying. I stared through bloodshot eyes at her demented, blubbering features and tried to tune in to what she was saying, thinking to myself: 'What? You and my dad? Something about some nuns? And a baby? What baby? Slow down, Mum, can't you see I'm stoned? Pete Townshend? What's he got to do with anything? Seriously, if you don't slow down, I think I'm gonna spew. I wonder if we've got any Yop in the fridge? That'd make everything seem better, some lovely Yop. And maybe a Twix.'

I shuffled off to the kitchen to check the fridge. There was no Yop. Then, all of a sudden, her mad flurry of words distilled in my head. I shuffled back into the living room and said, 'Sorry, did you just say that you had a baby with my dad when you were sixteen and then had it adopted?'

'Yes,' she whimpered.

It was the most earth-shattering news I'd ever heard. Remember, this was years before that whole John Major and Edwina Currie story broke.

I gave my mum a cuddle, and we talked about it for a bit longer. She filled me in on the salient details and explained that she'd never found the right time to tell me before. My brothers had found out a few years beforehand, when one of them had discovered Caroline's birth certificate among my mum's personal papers.

As you can imagine, my head was full of all sorts of thoughts after that. It wasn't dissimilar to how I felt after watching the revelatory denouement of *The Usual Suspects*, when my brain started racing back through every scene in the film, looking at it from a fresh perspective. Suddenly certain things made sense. Like the strange sense of sadness that always seemed to simmer beneath my mum's veneer of claptrap-spouting joviality. But mostly it intensified my sense of life's chaotic nature. This feeling had already been cultivated over the past nineteen years by all the cat-killing, loan sharks, stolen *Star Wars* figures, Gat-gun shoot-outs and other pathetic little incidents that had somehow impacted on my worldview. I looked on my mum and dad's story as impossibly romantic, terrifying, complicated and preposterous all at once. I kind of loved it and hated it at the same time. One thing was for sure: I didn't want to go through anything similar.

So about a year later I got together with the girl I'd had a crush on since I was at school. We fell in love, went to university together, then moved back to London, got jobs, got a mortgage, got married and had a baby. No adoptions, no nuns, no rock 'n' roll clubs and no involvements in speculative leftist *coups d'état*. The High Numbers never even made so much as a cameo appearance. Sure, there was the time we briefly got to party backstage with short-lived Liverpudlian Britpop sensations Space, but, other than that, we played life with a comparatively straight bat. I'd like to think I could raise my daughter in a more controlled environment than I was raised in. I've not got too many complaints about the way my parents treated me. My dad may have done the off, but at least he was a good bloke. Better a good dad that's absent than a shit one who sticks around. And at least I got to go to McDonald's more than the average kid. An estranged father will never turn down his kid's request for a Big Mac and fries. Back then a meal deal would have only cost about two pounds fifty – which is a small price to pay if you're a dad looking to ease a tiny part of his conscience. This is why kids from broken homes tend to be chubbier than those who live with both parents.

In short, living in a single-parent family isn't all bad. But had my dad been around more then I suppose there's a chance I'd have grown up to be less of a dumbo. He would have had a better chance of teaching me chess for starters. Not to mention the other stuff he would have liked to teach me. Like when he bought me a book on birdwatching and took me up Richmond Park with some binoculars. I liked the idea of doing that sort of stuff, I really did. I could envisage myself being one of those swotty kids who actually choose to do clever stuff outside school hours. But cultivating that sort of personality in a child is a full-time job. The odd weekend of cerebral pursuits here and there was never going to make a lasting impact on my fledgling brain. There was no way I was going to go home and crib up on the lesser spotted whitethroat during my own time when there was no one there hassling me to do so. With my mum at work, I was left to my own devices most of the time. If I wasn't trying to avoid being locked in the airing cupboard by my brothers, I liked to relax with a bowl of Instant Whip in front of the box. Or just while away a few hours melting polystyrene in the bathroom sink. I was very much a boy of simple pleasures.

As a result of my sedentary lifestyle, my worldview was largely shaped by whatever crap the TV or cinema served up. Fatherly role models were provided by Australian soaps or the teenage comedies of John Hughes. And king among all screen fathers was always, to my mind, Teen Wolf's dad. Still is. What wasn't there to love about him? For starters, he was a wolf. Second, he was a widower who managed to raise a troubled son single-handedly while simultaneously running his own small business. He was warm, dependable and cuddly. That scene where he appears at the bathroom door in wolf form to gently comfort his son, Michael J. Fox, is one of the most poignant moments of cinematic fatherliness ever committed to celluloid. Teen Wolf's dad is the dad I want to be. In fact, if I was even half the man Teen Wolf's dad was, then I'd be happy. But of course, *Teen Wolf* was just a film. And not a very realistic one if you think about it: I mean, why would being a werewolf necessarily make you better at playing basketball?

In real life I had no one remotely like Teen Wolf's dad serving as a role model. What I had were my older brothers. You've already heard enough about them to get the idea that they weren't exactly dedicated mentors. That said, they did once teach me how to play poker.

'Sam, d'you want us to teach you how to play our special card game?' they asked one evening with uncharacteristic enthusiasm. Even at the age of ten I was wily enough to know they must be up to something. And I knew what: they figured they could teach me the rudiments, get me hooked then clean out the contents of the Natwest Young Savers piggy bank that sat atop my bedroom cabinet containing about £7.80 in loose change. To me that represented a year's worth of saving towards my mum's Christmas present. To them it represented a sixteenth of an ounce of low-grade Lebanese hashish as sold by a bloke outside the Wimpy in Chiswick. Doesn't sound like much, but if they smoked it through a chillum, it could have put their brains out of action for a whole school week. Suffice to say, the stakes were pretty high.

My poker lesson amounted to little more than five minutes of them impatiently explaining how the hands worked. I tried to ask questions to clarify a few points, but it was too late: they were already dealing the cards and telling me that I'd pick it up as I went along. The first couple of hands went up to about 20 pence. Those were losses I could sustain. Soon there was a knock at the door, and some of their mates began to drift in. The living room filled up with cigarette smoke and the stench of budget lager. I felt slightly scared in a grown-up sort of a way. I lost another couple of hands, but the rules gradually started to make sense. Soon I was getting the hang of things. More importantly, I was getting dealt the right cards. I won a couple of hands for small change, and my brothers laughed it off. They probably told themselves it was all part of the hustle. But as the stakes grew, so did my confidence. I won a couple of quid. Then a fiver. I was beginning seriously to jeopardise my brothers' sixteenth of Leb and, even worse, was embarrassing them in front of their mates. Just to escalate matters, I decided to get a bit flashy.

'Come on, you wankers, this is getting a bit too easy,' I said as I flamboyantly lobbed another handful of change into the middle of the table, leaning back on my chair like I was Johnny Big Bucks. If this had been a western, they would have warned me about getting too sure of myself and gently implied that I should watch my smart mouth if I wanted to get out of there alive. But they were more blunt than that.

'Sam, here's the deal,' they said as I sat there taking an ostentatious swig from my celebratory glass of Vimto. 'If you win another hand like that, we're gonna kick your head in.'

Experience should have told me to take the threat seriously. But I was high on my own success. For a brief moment on that smoky evening in 1985 I thought I was immortal. So instead of saying 'Fair enough, chaps, that's perfectly understandable. Why don't you just take all the money back and I'll pop off to bed?' I fixed my oldest brother's stare with my best Clint Eastwood and said, 'Deal.'

I remember the exact moment I got dealt the fourth queen.

'Wait a minute, that's four of a kind!' I thought to myself gleefully. In fact, I think I may have actually muttered it out loud – I hadn't quite got to grips with the idea of a poker face yet. Luckily they were too drunk to hear me. Everyone had folded bar me and one of their mates.

'What's he got?' asked an onlooker nervously as I was forced to show my hand.

'Well,' slurred a brother as I reached to turn my final card over. 'He's got two queens showing. And I haven't seen any others so far. But I doubt he's got . . .'

'FOUR QUEENS!' I blurted before he could finish speculating. 'FOUR QUEENS! FOUR QUEENS! I've got four queens!'

My hands reached for the pile of cash sitting in the centre of the table. In the interests of dramatic effect I'd like to pretend there was a brief moment of silence as it dawned on me what was about to happen. But the truth is I didn't have time to think before the first shoe hit me. I remember hearing someone shout, 'Right, we fucking warned you,' and the rest is a blur of vintage '80s trainers descending on me as I lay curled up in the corner, clutching whatever winnings I had managed to grab and giggling with adrenalised fear.

So they did at least teach me some important lessons that day. They taught me to understand the consequences of my actions, never to get too cocky and that success brings its own challenges.

It may be unfair to say that that was the only lesson I ever received from them. My middle brother went through a brief boxing phase when he was in his teens. One day he came home and said that I needed toughening up. He dragged me upstairs to my mum's bedroom, where he turned the double bed into a makeshift ring. He spent a good hour teaching me how to jab, dodge and weave, followed by a futile ten minutes trying to teach me how to skip. Once that was over with, he announced it was time to put all I'd learned into action. We climbed on to the mattress – me on my feet, him on his knees to even things up.

'Right,' he said, 'remember everything I've told you. Keep your guard up and keep moving.'

'Is he serious?' I thought to myself. 'I haven't understood a word he's said for the past hour. I was happily sat in front of *Sunday Sunday* with Gloria Hunniford a minute ago, now I'm wobbling about on a mattress being made to fight a bloke twice my size.'

'Ding ding!' shouted my brother. Then he punched me in the mouth and I cried. That was the end of the lesson. He said I just wasn't cut out for boxing like he was.

The only other bloke who ever spent a prolonged period living at our place was Rab the milkman, whom my mum took up with when I was about nine. He was a gangly Scottish fella with a stupid bubble perm and a moustache, like a cross between the footballer Terry McDermott and Ronald McDonald. I found the fact that he was a milkman quite glamorous, and he would often let me join him on his morning rounds, when I would gain thrilling access to his Unigate Dairies float and all the precious bounty it carried. Among the dozens of silver- and gold-topped bottles there was always two crates of cartoned milk we carried especially for delivery to Feltham Young Offenders Institute.

'Why don't they get bottles like everyone else?' I asked Rab.

'Because they'd use the glass to try and kill themselves or each other,' he replied flatly. Suddenly the job seemed so dangerous and edgy, it was like I was doing work experience with Delta Force. There were other things that made Rab seem cool too, like the fact that he claimed to have once played professional football for Hibernian. Although now, of course, I realise that most of what he said was complete lies, and Rab was, in fact, a bit of a twat.

My brothers were old enough to appreciate this at the time. He generally made their lives a nightmare. Once he stumbled into the local pub where my oldest brother was having a drink with some mates. Rab slumped drunkenly beside them and, by means of an intro, sunk his teeth into one of their legs, drawing blood. When the others objected, Rab offered to fight them all. Eventually he grabbed my brother by the shoulder and insisted he return home to see his mum immediately.

Once home, Rab perked up.

'I'm home, hon!' he called out to my mum. 'And I've brought you your favourite.' He produced a thin carrier bag that he'd had stuffed down the front of his coat and emptied it on the coffee table. Out flopped two greasy, stone-cold doner kebabs.

My mum regarded them for a few seconds and asked, 'Are you drunk?'

Rab chuckled.

'Me? Drunk? I dunno what you're talking about, hon! I'm away upstairs for a quick pish. You get stuck into your kebab.'

And with that he staggered upstairs, vomited in the toilet and didn't emerge again for the rest of the evening. Shortly afterwards, my brother moved out and went to live with my dad.

'I was a semi-pro golfer, ya bastards!' Rab announced one night after another lengthy session down the local. We were sat watching telly and failing to treat his latest boast with sufficient respect. Before we knew it he had gone off to fetch his 9-iron from the cupboard under the stairs and was stood in front of the TV demonstrating his swing.

'I could be making a fortune on the tour if I wanted!' he insisted.

We shifted position to try and view the screen behind him. Eventually he snapped.

'Right, ya bastards! You're all coming with me to the park right now.'

He fetched a ball and a tee, and we were all marched reluctantly down to the local square. The fact that it was dark didn't seem to bother him; he assured us that he could make his golfing prowess apparent with just a single shot. He shakily pressed the tee into the grass, placed the ball on top and instructed us all to stand back. He spent a few minutes carefully positioning himself, then let fly. Only nothing really flew at all. He just skimmed the top of the ball, which trickled lamely about a yard in front of the tee. But Rab was oblivious: he stood with his hand to his brow like a ship's captain looking out to sea and cooed loudly: 'Jesus Christ! Did you see that, ya bastards? Must have sailed straight over those trees and outta the park!' With his vicious attack on my brother's mate's calf still fresh in our memories, we all thought it safer to gently applaud, then quickly head home.

He may have acted the hard man with us kids, but he was strangely petrified of my dad. Whenever my old man came round to pick me up at weekends, Rab would scuttle upstairs and hide in one of the bedrooms. Which was weird, because my dad didn't seem to have much of a problem with him at all. One Saturday afternoon Dad was dropping me off when I spotted Rab coming up the street the other way.

'Hey, look Dad, there's Rab!' I shouted, naively certain that the two men would be thrilled to see each other.

'Where? What are you talking about?' said my dad

irritably, looking around. I looked back, and Rab had disappeared.

'He was there a minute ago,' I insisted. Then I saw a movement beside a Ford Cortina parked at the side of the road. Squatting down beside it was Rab.

'There he is!' I said, assuming he must have dropped something. It didn't occur to me for a moment that Rab was hiding.

'Don't be ridiculous,' grumped my father. 'You're seeing things!'

I walked right up to the car and tried to address Rab but found him shuffling on his haunches around the other side.

'Rab, what are you doing?' I asked as he tried to shoo me away with a wave of his arm.

'Piss off!' he hissed, ducking his head. Looking back, I think my dad had cottoned on to what was happening but just couldn't bring himself to acknowledge the absurdity of the situation.

'Come on, there's nobody under the car, let's go inside,' he said. I left Rab, crouched and humiliated beside that Cortina, wondering to myself why he had told me to piss off.

Things came to a head for Rab a few months later. My middle brother was sixteen by now and had left school to become a postman. He worked shifts and would come home at strange hours of the day, tired, irritable and hungry. One afternoon he turned up to find Rab sprawled lazily on the sofa with an empty tub of raspberry ripple ice-cream beside him.

'I bought that ice-cream specially for my pudding when I got in from work!' my brother exploded.

'Well, don't blame me, son,' grinned Rab. 'That tub was sitting there empty when I got home from my round. Must've been someone else who ate it.' But my brother knew otherwise.

'You've still got bits of it in your stupid fucking moustache, you thieving cunt!' he spat, pointing an accusatory finger at the tell-tale drips around Rab's mouth. The row escalated quickly, and Rab jumped to his feet, taking a swing at my brother's head. My brother made off to the kitchen and came back waving my mum's biggest carving knife and telling him to get out of the house. Which he did. A few days after that he came back to collect his things, and then we never saw him again. We took ice-cream seriously in our house.

I'm changing the baby's nappy on the living-room floor.

'You're not doing that right,' says my dad, peering over me.

'In what way?' I ask.

'In every way,' he replies.

'This is the way I always do it,' I insist. 'It seems to work fine.'

'Well, why is she crying her eyes out then?'

'Because babies cry their eyes out. Don't they?'

'They do if you change their nappy like that.'

I wait for him to tell me how I should be changing the nappy. But he just looks at his watch and says, 'Shit, my pay-and-display is about to run out. I've got to go.'

I decide to remove the nappy I had already stuck on her arse and start again. There is a short interim period between the old nappy being removed and the new one being fitted, during which she fires a yellowish projectile shit across the room like a rocket. It hits the wall next to the plasma and starts to drip down apologetically. It looks a bit like chicken korma. I quickly wipe her up and attach the new nappy. Then I start to scrub the shit from the wall. And d'you know what? I don't really stop to think how my dad, my brothers, Rab or even Teen Wolf's dad would approach the situation. I just keep scrubbing until the shit has disappeared. Only it never does. But it does at least fade to a faint stain, which I reckon will be almost unnoticeable in dim lighting.

14

TWAT

My wife hears me calling the baby a twat on the baby monitor.

'You can't call the baby a twat!' she says through the speaker from downstairs.

'But she's acting like one!' I explain. 'She keeps pretending to be asleep, then waking up and screaming when I try to put her down. She's playing mind games.'

My wife comes upstairs. She looks disappointed. Stupid baby monitor.

'Look, I wouldn't have called her a twat, had I known you were listening,' I reason.

'What kind of excuse is that?'

'Well, it's only you who's offended by it. To her ears it's just a noise.'

'That's not the point.'

'Yes it is. She can't even understand her own name yet – how's she supposed to know that "twat" is a rude word?'

'I'm not worried about you offending her. I'm worried about her first word being "twat".'

I look down at the baby's tiny, scrunched-up face. She doesn't look anywhere near ready to talk yet. Whenever she does open her mouth, all that comes out is a croaky sort of belch and a splat of thin, white puke.

'Are you asking me to stop swearing in front of the baby?' I ask in disbelief.

'That's exactly what I'm asking you to do,' she says.

'But swearing is my release!' I protest. 'Think yourself lucky. For some blokes it's glue.'

She takes the baby from my arms, giving me a dirty look as if I was some sort of abusive father. Next thing I know, she's announced a blanket ban on all potty mouthing. I'm not allowed to swear at or in front of the baby. It's like Mao's fucking China round here. Ha! Can't stop me writing my precious swear words down, can you? No baby monitor to spy on me while I write, is there?

In the night the baby cries and cries and cries. My wife feeds her, and she shuts up for, like, ten minutes. Then, just as we're drifting back towards sleep, she starts up again. Maybe she needs burping? Maybe she's too hot? Maybe she's had a bad dream? Maybe she's worried about the situation in Gaza? I don't bloody know. There's no way of knowing. She is less communicative than a pot plant. You'd have more luck asking a cactus what the matter was.

But we can at least try to find a way of making it stop. In the depths of the night we blearily sing her songs, walk her round, put a finger in her mouth for her to suck on.

'Maybe she needs winding?' one of us mumbles.

We try an elaborate succession of methods to elicit a burp. First we lay her over our shoulders and stroke her back. That doesn't work, so we hold her to our chest, facing outwards, with the palm of our hands resting on her stomach. Still no dice. My wife doesn't let me try the more elaborate ones that require above-average dexterity. 'You'll gouge out her eyeball or something,' she reasons.

Every parent we know has a different winding method that they claim is fail-safe. A sister-in-law teaches us one where you sit the baby upright on your knee, grab her by the face and rotate her head in vigorous circles. It proves the most effective so far. She burps twice after about thirty seconds. It's also funny to watch. I film it on my mobile phone and show it to my dad when he comes round.

'Jesus, it looks like you're . . . you're strangling her,' he says in horror. I look back at the footage, sniggering. It really does look like she's being strangled. I stop sniggering. It reminds me of those dehumanising torture rituals you see US troops subjecting Iraqi prisoners to. We decide not to ever do it again, however effective it seems.

In the night she sleeps in a basket next to our bed. She wakes up needing a feed every two hours. I have no real role to play in this but feel I ought at least to wake up and give some moral support. Over the past few weeks I have trained myself to sit upright and blurt out 'Do you need any help? Sure? OK, goodnight' without actually waking up.

Sometimes, only occasionally, she goes straight back to sleep after her feed. I lie in bed listening out for her breathing. I am unsettled by the eerie silence. I have to get out of bed, creep over to her basket and rest my hand on her chest to check her lungs are moving.

'What are you doing?' my wife asks, waking up with a start.

'I'm checking that she's still breathing,' I say. 'I thought she might be dead.' The baby wakes up and starts to cry.

I pick her up and walk her round the bedroom. She keeps on crying. I walk her up and down the stairs. She keeps on crying. I stick a badger-shaped glove puppet on my hand and start saying 'Barry Badger doesn't like it when you cry' in what I consider to be a hilarious badger voice. She cries even louder. My wife calls out from the bedroom: 'Stop doing the badger voice. She doesn't like it.'

I walk into the bathroom and switch on the light. The fan starts to make a whirring sound. She stops crying! She likes the sound of the fan. Maybe it reminds her of being inside the womb. It's not what I imagined it would sound like inside a woman. I'd always thought their innards echoed with the sexy whine of a jazz saxophonist. This is more of a mechanical, monotonous drone. But who cares? I have found a way of stopping the crying. I have broken the Enigma code of my baby's tear ducts.

The next night I am lying in bed, unable to sleep again. I get up and check that she is breathing again. She wakes up again.

'For fuck's sake!' says my wife.

'Don't swear in front of the baby!' I say.

She chucks the badger puppet at me. I pick the baby up and head for the bathroom.

'I'll have this sorted in a jiffy,' I announce confidently. I walk into the bathroom and switch on the light. She keeps on crying. The fan starts to whirr. She keeps on crying.

'Can't you hear the fan?' I ask her. 'It's nice, isn't it? It's like being inside Mummy's tummy.' She keeps on crying. She makes out she doesn't know what I'm on about. See what I mean? Twat.

This carries on for weeks. Time and time again she fools me into thinking I've found the magic formula to stop her crying. Time and time again my hopes are dashed. In the dead of night I take her downstairs and switch on the TV. She keeps crying while I surf through the channels. When I get to Price Drop TV, she stops suddenly. She is captivated by a young female presenter eulogising about a vegetable steamer. Maybe it's the soothing tones of the presenter's sales patter. Or the orangey glow of her complexion. Perhaps it's the steamer itself that has caught her eye. Certainly, £18.99 for a device that cooks a whole family meal at that speed seems like exceptional value. Price Drop TV appears to be the answer to my prayers. I hit the Sky Plus button so I can show her the same bit again the next night. But of course she's gone off the orangey host and her vegetable steamer by then. She's gone off Price Drop TV altogether. So I surf some more. Eventually we land on Muslim TV. Her jaw drops, and she falls silent. After ten minutes of watching she nods off to sleep. I say a little prayer of thanks to Allah.

By the next night she's so over Islam. She's fickle. Her attention span makes mine look positively vast. Soon she's gone off the idea of telly altogether. Within a week I'm standing in the kitchen at half-past three in the morning repeatedly flicking the lights on and off like a strobe while jumping up and down on the spot. It's a bit like being at a rave, only really quiet and lonely and depressing. But it's what seems to work today.

'Please stop crying,' I plead with her in a whisper on one of the nights when none of the tricks seems to be working. I have reached breaking point. I feel like sobbing. All I want is a sleep. In fact, a sleep would be an indulgence. A nap would do. A snooze would be luxury. I'd sell both my kidneys for a humble doze. I am practically on my knees begging her to give it a rest.

'I'll buy you a pony if you just stop crying,' I whimper. She just looks straight through me like I wasn't even there.

Her pious resistance to bribery is starting to irritate me. And it's not just bribery either: all of the techniques I usually employ to get my own way with people just don't wash with her.

First I try rational appeals.

'You're only crying because you're tired,' I explain gently. 'And the more you cry, the more tired you'll get. Can't you see? It's all just a vicious circle.' She screams until snot comes out of her nose. She's not ready to listen to reason. So I start to pull out a few dirty tricks.

'Oh, you're crying!' I sneer at her. 'How very mature of you. What a constructive course of action!'

But sarcasm is pointless. So I give mockery a go.

'Waaahh! Waaahh! Ooh, I'm a big baby! I can't stop crying! My life's so hard! Coz all I do all day is sit around drinking milk and having my arse wiped!' It's all like water off a duck's back to her.

As a final throw of the dice I become aggressive.

'Are you gonna stop crying, or is daddy going to have to get very angry with you?' I ask menacingly.

'Remember what we said about threatening the baby?' says my wife. I didn't even know she was listening. Stupid baby monitor.

*

These nightly exchanges are bringing my limited interpersonal skills into sharp focus. These techniques are pretty much all I've ever used to get my own way with people. I try to be reasonable, but that doesn't work with everyone. Sometimes I patronise. Occasionally I condescend. From time to time I do that thing of just repeating whatever someone says back to them. But, you know, in a silly voice. And once in a while I just put my hands over my ears, turn around and walk away. I use these tricks at work; I use them against my wife; I've even used them to hurry up waiters with my dessert. They are tried and tested. They work.

In fact, they're wasted on the trivial conflicts thrown up by everyday life. Imagine the impact they could have in a court of law or on the diplomatic circuit. Palestine? I'd turn up and do a load of quite cruel yet funny impressions of delegates from both sides. It'd lighten the mood and put the senselessness of all that bloodshed into sudden perspective. Northern Ireland? I'd probably use a bit of light sarcasm to lampoon the folly of sectarianism. Tibet? I'd patronise the Chinese into submission. If that didn't work, I might turn aggressive. I'd find a way somehow. I'm a persuasive person.

That's what I always thought anyway. But this baby is impervious to my powers. I just can't break her down. No amount of words will help. It's unnerving, because words are all I have. Flannel and chatter are usually my answer to everything. Without them I am helpless.

She's not trying to point-score. There's no argument to win here. She's got no agenda for me to expose and belittle. She is just genuinely distressed. And I have to find a way of making her better. It's intimidating. So I pick her up, I cuddle her, I let her suck my finger and I go into the kitchen and start flicking the lights on and off. And I learn to keep my mouth shut. Most of the time.

I also learn this: babies just cry. I can sometimes hear the one from two doors down wailing its guts up in the night. I see loads of the little bastards in their pushchairs up the high street bawling away. They're all at it. It comes naturally to them. There doesn't have to be a reason, beyond the fact that they've suddenly been awakened from a peaceful nine-month slumber, dragged out of the comfort of a nice warm womb and chucked unceremoniously into the noisy, colourful, stinking world. It's disorientating and scary. In adult terms it'd be like being snatched from your comfy bed in the dead of night, blindfolded, slung in a van, driven up to Hartlepool and booted through the doors of a Yates Wine Lodge into the middle of a local hen night's lock-in. You couldn't run away, because your legs wouldn't work. You couldn't call for help, because you wouldn't know how to speak. So you'd just sit there and cry and cry and cry. And not even Price Drop TV could make you stop. That's what being born must feel like. Being born is rubbish.

So where's my motivation? If you don't have kids of your own, you may be wondering why I'm putting up with all this. Why I didn't just grab my toothbrush, hot-foot it to Heathrow and catch the first flight to Fiji after the first few nights of torture? Well, listen to this: eventually she nods off. I mean, she has to in the end, doesn't she? And then, just before I do the same, I find myself staring at her face. It has quickly turned from red and tear-stained to delicate and peaceful. Her nose is tiny and perfect. Her skin is smooth like ivory. Her soft, dark hair frames her tiny, beautiful features. Can you see what's happening here? I'm turning all poetic and soppy. That's what happens every single night. All the pain and suffering she's put me through are just washed away in seconds. Everything inside my body is pleading with me to shut my eyes and go to sleep, but I can't. I just keep staring. And I feel all proud and warm and happy inside. It's like the worst sort of all-consuming crush. Don't worry, I'm not actually going to write a poem; it's not that bad.

I don't suppose there's anything exceptional about this response. God must have made us this way. Only I don't believe in God, so I suppose it must be the upshot of some complex process of evolution that you could trace back to the paternal conduct of giant turtles on the Galapagos or something.

The days are a walk in the park by comparison. Some babies seem to keep the crying up 24/7, but we've been lucky. Ours just sleeps, feeds and occasionally opens her eyes really wide and stares into space for fifteen minutes or so. That's what passes for a moment of genuine excitement in our household these days. If we're lucky, she'll even contort her little mouth into an amusing 'O' shape while she's staring. That's when you have to cry out in excitement to whoever else is in the house: 'Come quickly! You'll never fucking believe what's happening! She's staring into space while pulling an unusual facial expression! Get the camera!'

'Do we really have to be one of those twee families who go around saying stuff like "sugar" and "fiddlesticks"?' I ask my wife during the baby's afternoon nap. This swearing issue has been playing on my mind. 'What are you going to do next? Ban us from watching ITV? Make us eat brown bread?'

'If you swear in front of her all the time, she'll grow up foul-mouthed,' she says.

'Don't be stupid. There were no swearing restrictions in my family and look at us – dead eloquent.'

'Sam, you're niece's first word was "cunt".'

That shuts me up.

My wife doesn't mind a good swear herself, but she's not as committed as I am. There was no swearing in her house when she was growing up. She was too busy having piano lessons and playing with wooden, educational toys to be bothered with foul-mouthed experimentation. It wasn't that her parents were particularly strict. I suppose her household was just so pleasant that there was never any call to resort to nasty words. I imagine that she might have let the occasional 'flipping hell' slip out during heated games of Pictionary. Other than that, it was all pretty polite.

Round my house it was total foul-mouthed anarchy. My mum would never use one swear word when five of them strung together into a hybrid super-swear word would do. 'Shitfuckingwankfacetosser!' we'd hear her scream to herself after we'd displeased her in some way. 'Fuck it all! Fuck it all!' she would squawk in a kind of demented sing-song while clearing up the mess from another unsanctioned party. Sometimes these wild-eyed sing-songs would be mostly swearless but rich in berserk sarcasm: 'I luuuuuurve my life!' she'd warble or, bizarrely,

'You're the creeeaam in my cofffeeeee!' To be fair, she rarely swore directly at us. Usually she seemed to be screaming at the heavens, angrily holding God to account for the unmanageable predicament he'd landed her in.

I've got to admit, there was a certain eloquence to mum's mental outbursts. She laces words together – sweary or otherwise – with a poetic vim.

Once, when I was about eleven, my mate Joe was round playing with *Star Wars* figures in the living room. My brother came back from his shift at the post office and started rowing with my mum in the kitchen about unpaid housekeeping or something. Joe started to look a bit concerned, so I tried to distract him by zooming my replica Millennium Falcon round his head, making laser-gun noises. Suddenly there was a loud smash, and the pair of us ran into the hallway to see what was happening. My brother had lobbed his baked spud and beans against the kitchen wall. Between them they had wrecked the place. There was orange tomato sauce and bits of broken plate everywhere.

'Shit fire!' screeched my mother, which was a trademark phrase of hers. 'You fucking little shit arse!'

Poor old Joe's face went all pale and disturbed. It wasn't like he hadn't heard swearing before. I don't suppose he'd heard it come out of a mum's gob before, though. She ran screaming out of the house. My brother kicked a chair over, punched a dent in the door and stormed off in the opposite direction. I was dead embarrassed. When Joe's mum came round to pick him up, she politely asked where the adults were and why there were baked beans everywhere. Joe said he'd explain on the way home.

It got so I was barely able to distinguish between polite and impolite language. I knew the 'F' and 'C' words were not to be used in civilised company but, beyond that, I didn't have a clue. There was teacher at primary school who coached the football team who was often willing to indulge us in a bit of matey footballing banter. One day, in a misjudged bit of dressing-room larking, I told him to 'bugger off'. I had no idea what it meant, but it struck me as quite a grown-up, old-fashioned sort of a phrase, the sort of thing a teacher would almost admire you for using. I was wrong. The bastard whacked me round the back of the head with his clipboard. 'But "bugger" isn't swearing, sir!' I insisted. I never made the first team after that.

My dad was similarly perturbed by my foul effing and jeffing whenever I visited his home on weekends. Once, when I was about seven, I upset him by casually commenting that it was 'pissing down' outside. I didn't have a clue that he was objecting to the word 'pissing'. I thought he was just upset about the weather. Even when he explained it to me, I chose to argue the toss with him. 'Piss? Ha! That's not swearing!' I insisted. Which only made things worse. No one likes a seven-year-old trying to outwit them in a semantic debate.

In the summer, he would usually take us on holiday, where he would learn, over the course of a fortnight in our company, the full extent of his offspring's unsavoury manners. He seemed ever so disappointed. We were all in a hire car in Portugal once when I whimsically enquired from the back seat: 'What's a poofter?' My dad and his missus exchanged uncomfortable glances, and my brothers started to grin.

'It's a derogatory term for a homosexual', my dad explained in terms I had no chance of understanding.

One of my brothers ill-advisedly tried to alleviate the awkward atmosphere that ensued by piping up: 'Yes, like "turd burglar".' He later told me that he wasn't quite sure what 'turd burglar' actually meant, but he'd recently heard a mate use it and saw that moment in the car as the perfect opportunity to give it a run-out. It was an error of judgement.

My dad stopped the car and clipped him round the ear, barking, 'That's enough of that!' I was nonplussed. The lexicon of homophobia remained a mystery to me. A few months later an old family friend came round for lunch with his boyfriend, and I thought nothing of referring to them as 'turd burglars' to their faces. Which just goes to show the pitfalls of brushing swear words under the carpet.

'A kid should understand that swear words are very powerful. And that with great power comes great responsibility,' I suggest to my wife hopefully.

'That's from *Spiderman*,' she points out.

'What I'm saying is, kids will hear swear words whether you like it or not,' I continue. 'The best you can do is tell them what they mean and let them make their own mind up.'

'Oh really? And what are you going to tell our daughter when she asks you what "twat" means?'

'Not sure. It means "fanny", doesn't it? Or does it?'

None of this tackles the sticky business of my niece and the 'C' word. I'd only been going out with my wife for a few months when I convinced her to come on a family holiday to Ireland with my mum and my brothers and their wives. My youngest brother had his daughter in tow, who was just walking. It was an ugly fortnight, characterised by violent rows and heavy drinking. It was no place for a new girlfriend, let alone a child. My wife spent the whole time looking a bit shell-shocked by the general hullabaloo and antagonism that permeated those long days spent in quaint fishing village boozers. We argued constantly over the sort of stuff that I suppose all brothers argue about: long-disputed Subbuteo matches mostly. Occasionally my mum would burst into tears. Maddy, my tiny, cherubic niece, would merrily totter around the place, seemingly oblivious to the menacing climate. One day my wife turned to me, looking even more ashen-faced than usual.

'What is it?' I slurred.

'Maddy just said "cunt",' she replied.

'What?' I said, looking all confused and patting Maddy on her little blonde head. 'Naaah! She can't even talk, can you darling?'

'Cunt!' squeaked Maddy back at me.

It sounds funny written down, but it didn't seem so nice when you actually witnessed it. That ugly word spilling out of a face so angelic was a disconcerting thing to behold, I can tell you. Maddy had no sense of the power wielded by this exciting new term. But she'd been exposed to its persistent usage for over a week and was now repeating it back like a parrot. Which I guess makes my missus the winner of our argument. If I keep calling the baby a twat, it'll only be a matter of time before she calls me one back. Which will be justified but nonetheless distressing.

'OK, you're right, I suppose,' I concede to my wife. 'But that wasn't Maddy's first word. She was about three years old,' I add, making sure I at least scored some sort of pathetic consolation point.

I go upstairs and stand over the baby's cot watching her sleep. I stare at her gorgeous, innocent little face and try to imagine it saying the 'C' word. I don't like it. I find it much easier to imagine her waking up suddenly, looking me straight in the eye and saying 'Daddy!' Or perhaps 'Morning!' Or even 'Rosebud!' in a weird, drawn-out croak. But, please, not 'cunt'. Never 'cunt'.

It's the next morning.

'Mummy,' I say, holding the baby in front of my face and doing the special baby voice. My wife carries on reading her posh-looking book. Something about a blind woman's plight in a prisoner-of-war camp, I shouldn't wonder.

'Muuuuummmy!' I persist.

'What is it?' she finally relents with a sigh.

'Daddy broke the swearing ban . . .'

A long pause.

'What did he say?'

'He called you a wanker. I think you should divorce him.' I keep the baby suspended in front of my grinning face.

'Maybe I will,' says my wife.

15

WORK

I peep through the blinds at the world outside. As the sunlight hits my eyes, I flinch and make a strange hissing sound. Resentfully, I peer at the birds, the trees, the litter. And the people. All those bastard people. 'Look at them with their routines and their jobs and their . . . lives,' I think to myself. 'I was once like them.' It's all just a distant memory now. I've been cocooned in this house for weeks. Or is it months? Hard to say. I know the baby has already outgrown certain items of clothing. This is what I've been reduced to: working out the passing of time by reference to clothing labels. Calendars are pretty much pointless to me. If someone asked me what the date was, I'd tell them it was roughly three to six months.

My chin is stubbly, and my eyes are drooping. I've worn tracksuit bottoms to the shops eight days running. I live off a diet of cake and tea. At first this lifestyle seemed novel. Then it became frustrating. But lately I've entered into the strangest phase of all: I'm actually starting to enjoy it. I've been institutionalised. I can barely imagine going back to civvy street now. From my vantage point at the bedroom window it all seems so hectic. Why is everyone in such a hurry? Feed time isn't for another hour and three-quarters.

But of course, those people – 'the others', I call them – don't care about feed time. What do they care about? What matters in the outside world? My mind strains to remember, but it's no use. All that matters to it now are the simple routines that prevail between these four walls. It really is like prison, just as I had envisaged: we spend long periods confined to our sleeping quarters (although, like Cat A prisoners on suicide watch, we are rarely allowed to actually sleep). There are regimented mealtimes. We slop out eight or nine times a day. I feel like 'fresh fish', a naive and petrified new inmate struggling to survive. My wife is a firm but fair warden. Which makes my daughter 'the daddy', calling the shots from inside her well-appointed cell.

Yes, it's so much simpler in here. Meanwhile, 'the others' continue to scurry around with implausible urgency outside. What *is* it that they're so preoccupied with? Slowly it starts to drift back to me. That look of concentration and mild panic in their eyes. The way they look at their precious 'watches' to see what 'time' it is. The fact that they've bothered to shave and put on proper clothes. Yes, that's it, they're going to work. I remember work. It once seemed so important. I had ambitions. I had five-year plans. I had places to go, people to see, meetings to doze through and colleagues to secretly despise. Those colleagues probably wouldn't recognise me if they saw me now, standing at the window with a baby in one hand and a slice of lemon drizzle cake in the other, naked but for a pair of loose-fitting karate pants. In their narrow-minded perceptions I may seem like a drop-out, a failure or a tramp. But the truth is, I am liberated. I have stepped back, seen the bigger picture and chosen to say 'no' to the social conventions that dictate the way they live. Why should I hit deadlines and change my pants every day just because that's what 'The Man' says I should do? Screw The Man! I refuse to line his pockets any longer. I am happy here with my wife, my daughter and my prison fantasy. Today I shall spend my afternoon hand-washing shit-stained baby-grows using a bar of Vanish in the bathroom sink. I'm living the dream.

'Have you seen this American Express bill?' says my wife, wandering into the room. She has been doing paper-work downstairs. She said she wanted to keep her mind active. I knew it would end in tears. Opening the mail always does. And once you actually start to read it, you're just asking for trouble.

'Bills? Ha! They're of no relevance to us any more!' I want to tell her. 'Leave those to the squares and the bread heads! I do not recognise mainstream society's oppressive "billing system". From now on we shall get by using a simple bartering process with other like-minded parents from the local area. Either that or eBay. Either way, shut up about the bill.'

But I don't say any of that stuff. I just stand and gawp while she starts to read out some choice highlights of my expenditure in the months leading up to the birth.

'A hundred and fifty quid on a lunch . . . what the fuck?'

'It was important. It was to do with work. Or something.'

'A grand at Harvey Nichols? What for?'

'Erm, trousers. And some speciality cheeses.'

'Five hundred quid cash withdrawal from a service station in Chesterfield.'

'That was a bet that went wrong.'

She looks concerned. I'm a bit shaken up. That piece of paper is like a portal into the past life that I'd all but forgotten. A life of foolish decadence in which I spent money as a means of passing time. It became a hobby, like crochet or bridge. Only much more expensive and destructive to the soul.

I don't want you to think that that was my full-time lifestyle. I don't ordinarily prance about like the King of Siam, dining on swan flesh sandwiches, swigging thirstily from bejewelled goblets of monkey blood and buying socks fashioned from puppy-dog hair. But a few months before the baby came along my cousin Bruce gave me a bit of advice.

'Being a dad takes away the spontaneity from your life,' he said. 'You can't just go out and get spannered on a whim any more. And you have to start thinking twice about spending sprees. So make sure you cram a bit of that in before it's too late.'

Which correlated well with the advice Dave had given me less articulately a week or two beforehand. You know, about going out and getting twatted.

Well, I didn't need telling three times. On Bruce and Dave's recommendations I went berserk with my credit card, descending quickly into a horrific cesspit of greed and excess. I took myself out to lunch at nice restaurants while my wife was at work. I'd sit there alone like some weirdo scoffing starters, desserts, glasses of wine – the lot. Even coffee. I don't even like wine or coffee. I spent an afternoon in the Apple store splurging on attachments, some of which I still haven't opened. Scriptwriting software for my laptop? Like I'm going to write a flipping script. Who was I trying to kid? A device that claims to make you run faster if you plug it into your iPod? A printer that fits in your inside pocket? Most of it got lost in the move, still in their wrappers. That wasn't even the worst of it: I became the sort of bloke who, when buying a round of drinks in the pub, came back with loads of bags of crisps that nobody had even asked for. Yes, it really was that insane. As the memories of gargantuan bar bills and three-figure taxi meters start to stack up in my mind, I begin to feel dizzy.

'How much does it all come to?' I ask hesitantly.

'A few grand,' she says casually. 'Plus there's this month's mortgage and your VAT bill to pay. We've got all that covered, right?'

'Hahaha!' I blurt as a delaying tactic.

'Pardon?'

'I mean, yes! Of course! No problem!' I've sat down on the bed now and placed the sleeping baby beside me. I put the remains of the lemon drizzle cake on her tummy. I've suddenly lost my appetite.

'By the way,' I say in my best la-di-da, it-doesn't-really-matter-but-I-just-thought-I'd-ask-anyway sort of voice, 'you're still on full pay from work, right?'

'Only for another month,' she says. 'Then it drops to half.' Rubbish, stupid, useless maternity cover.

I give her the baby and go off to the toilet to clutch my head and make a high-pitched whining sound in panic. All of my idealistic notions about opting out of the rat race disintegrate in seconds. I need to get back to work. What was I thinking, just hanging around the house for weeks on end whistling 'Baa Baa Black Sheep'? Since when did responsible fathers act like that? It's like I just forgot to earn a living. Like I became some sort of . . . of . . . *hippy*. Thank Christ for that AmEx bill! I've been snapped back into a state of moral decency and capitalist gusto as fast as you could say 'repayment deferrals'.

I know, I know. My wife should probably be more keenly aware of our financial predicament. But it's impossible for me to keep her abreast of my earnings, because it's impossible for me to keep abreast of them myself. I haven't had a proper salary in almost ten years. I am 'self-employed'. To you, that may just sound like code for 'I get to masturbate about six or seven times a day', but it's more complicated than that. I call myself a journalist, but there's all sorts of things I do to earn money. Maybe the best way to illustrate my professional life is to outline my working week in the lead-up to the birth of my daughter.

On the Monday I was booked to appear on a weekly news review show on ITV. I would be part of a three-person panel of 'experts' who discussed the week's biggest news stories from a moral perspective. I know: I didn't have a clue what that meant either. But if you're a self-employed person, you can't afford to be too sniffy about what sort of employment you undertake. My policy is: if the people offering to pay me think I'm able to do it, then I might as well take their word for it. Only on this occasion I was probably wrong to do so. I'd got accidentally drunk the night before. Really drunk. The sort of drunk that makes you wake up the next morning feeling like you've been raped by a gorilla. I'm not usually so unprofessional as to get that twatted the night before a job, but we weren't supposed to be filming until two in the afternoon. Anyone can sober up and get themselves shipshape by that time of day, right? Wrong. I woke up bleary-eyed at midday. I cursed my cousin Bruce for setting me along this path of incessant revelry. I got a call from the TV producers saying my cab would be arriving at one. I checked through my e-mails to remind myself what the topics of discussion would be on the show. 'Let's hope for something nice and easy,' I thought to myself. 'A story about shortening hem-lines or obese children or the weather . . . something that I can just wing my way through.' Finally I stumbled on an e-mail headed 'Zimbabwe Special'. My head throbbed. My temples spewed out a sudden projection of sweat. I went to the toilet and threw up. Zimbabwe? In this state? I wasn't sure it was possible. I skimmed the BBC website. I cribbed some background on Wikipedia. I considered calling the producers and making something up about the death of a relative – probably Bruce, seeing as it's him I choose to blame for all of this. I went back to the toilet and threw up again. Then my cab arrived.

It wasn't so bad in the end. I stuck a tie on in the car. The make-up lady worked wonders with my complex-ion. Once we started filming, I nodded in the right places, stroked my chin where necessary, regurgitated a few opinions I'd read online at what I assumed were the cor-rect junctures and managed to squeeze in a facetious remark at the end to lighten the mood a little. All in all, a decent day's work done under difficult circumstances. I came away with a few hundred quid in my pocket, not sure whether to curse or thank silly old Robert Mugabe for the indirect part he had played in the afternoon's proceedings.

The next day I found myself alone in a tiny, darkened room saying these words over and over again in a really loud, stupid voice: 'This summer, find fun . . . find friendship . . . find family!' On the screen a cartoon fish danced about to the rhythm of some sort of underwater calypso party. In my headphones a voice kept saying, 'Could you try that again with more warmth this time please?' I sat up straight, clutched my script with added purpose and tried again. 'Fffffind fffun . . . ffffinf fffriendship . . . fffind fffamily.' I stared through the glass window at the producer.

'How's that? Any warmer?' I asked.

'Erm, it just sounded like you dragged out the 'F's more, to be honest,' he said, not unreasonably. 'Can we go again one more time? Remember, this is for kids, so let's really try to ramp up the fun, yeah?'

I was doing a voice-over to help promote a film about an animated family of dancing fish. I think the producer and I both knew he'd booked the wrong voice-over artist. I don't really do warmth. Or fun. I'm not sure what I do. My voice sounds a bit like a cat being savaged by a fox. Or, at best, like the sort of fifteen-year-old schoolboy who shouts 'Fuck off, mister' at you for no reason from the top window of a double-decker bus when you're trying to mind your own business on a provincial high street somewhere in the south-east of England. People close to me have described my voice variously as 'idiotic', 'grating', 'obnoxious' and 'fucking annoying'. But in the TV voice-over business it's considered 'urban' apparently, and that seems to be all the rage right now. The producer eventually decided that we'd achieved something in the vicinity of 'warmth' and let me go home.

On the Wednesday I went to interview Girls Aloud for a magazine at a photo studio in east London. They were dead nice. At the end of the day I asked if we could all have a picture taken together.

'Where are you off to now?' asked Cheryl Cole as we lined up for the snapper.

'Off home to check on my missus. She's due to give birth any day now,' I said.

'Oh, that's lovely, congratulations!' she said in her lovely Geordie voice. The others joined in the cooing. I felt proud.

'Just think, if it happens tonight, I'll always be able to tell my kid that I was with Girls Aloud on the day it was born!' I said.

I don't know why I said that. It was just a foolish moment of excited reverie, I suppose. As soon as the words left my mouth, a weird, awkward atmosphere fell over the room. A minute beforehand I'd had the sense we might all stay in touch and become friends. Now I could see them all exchanging funny glances like I'd weirded them out a bit. I suppose it did sound a bit nerdy and stalkerish. I felt embarrassed and went home.

The next day I took part in a documentary for BBC Three about the history of the word 'cunt'.

And on the Friday I went to Birmingham to film a series I was supposed to be fronting about crime in the UK. I was interviewing a young drug dealer called Carl when I received a text from my wife telling me that her waters had broken. I told Carl what had happened and explained that I had to go home right away. He wasn't happy that I was cutting short his fleeting moment of fame.

'What the fuck are you saying, blood?' he said. 'Finish the interview first. You're being disrespectful.' His hand kept fishing inside his jacket as if he had a knife or something in there. I was conflicted. On the one hand I knew I should really get home to be with my wife. On the other hand I didn't want to upset Carl in case he stabbed me. I could see the headlines flashing though my brain: 'Obscure television reporter stabbed to death after prematurely ending interview with drug lord.' Wouldn't have made much of an epitaph, would it? In the end, a producer stepped in and distracted Carl with some fancy TV double-speak while I snuck off to the station.

So there you have it: five days that give a pretty fair reflection of a working life that could be politely described as 'portfolio', less politely described as 'louche' and more accurately described as 'irresponsible and stupid'. I mean, I love my work. It's good fun. I don't have to go into an office very often, I rarely do the same thing two days running, and I don't have a boss telling me what to do. Sometimes, if I really feel like it, I can cancel stuff and spend a whole day watching my box set of *Dick Turpin* DVDs, starring Richard O'Sullivan. Who could complain about a life like that? The fact that I have no pension, no sick pay, no paid holidays, little in the way of savings and absolutely nothing in the way of security never really bothered me before. I was sticking it to the system. And if things ever really did go tits up, then what did I stand to lose? My home maybe. But I'd thought long and hard about life as a hobo, and I reckoned I could handle it. Those long nights stood round a burning oil drum. The all-day, guilt-free drinking binges. It actually seemed like good fun. I'd grow a beard and learn to play the harmonica. I think my marriage is solid enough to survive a few years of vagrancy. My wife would stick by me and become a she-tramp with leaves wrapped round her feet and pants made from a Tesco carrier bag. We'd be the couple you saw fighting over a can of Special Brew in the park. It'd be romantic. And from time to time I'm sure people would still give me the odd day's work. I might not get so much of the on-camera stuff, but I'm sure I could still write the odd book review or perform the occasional voice-over. I mean, you don't get much more 'urban' than a tramp, do you?

But things are different now. I have a daughter to look after. The overheads are low at the moment – she feeds for free from her mother's boobies and dresses mostly in hand-me-down all-in-ones. But I expect it won't be long before she's demanding sweeties or a Stretch Armstrong or a deposit on a studio flat in Shoreditch. I can't allow her to fall into vagrancy in the meantime. No one likes to see a tramp-baby, do they? Mind you, the thought of her growing up as some sort of cheeky Dickensian street urchin is not entirely unappealing. Scurrying up chimneys, shining the shoes of the upper classes, performing the Lambeth Walk in her raggedy trousers in return for a shiny ha'penny piece. They say economic meltdown is just around the corner. The return of the traditional English guttersnipe may well be one of the few consolations.

Nevertheless, a dad shouldn't tit about interviewing pop bands for a living. A dad should be out on the seven o'clock train doing the *Times* crossword. He should have a brolly under his arm and a big promotion on his mind. I'm thirty-two – I should have a personal assistant and one of those intercom boxes on my desk by now. As it is, I don't even have a desk. I've got a dining table covered in unopened mail and old newspapers that I balance my laptop on whenever I have to write. The other day I tried to type an article one-handed while holding the baby in my other arm. Every time I tried to hit the space bar I banged her head on the table. This confronted me with a tricky conundrum: complete the article and give the baby concussion or stop and set in motion a sequence of events that could ultimately let her starve. In the end I just dumped her on the floor and let her scream for ten minutes while I finished the article very quickly to a below-par standard. Which was probably the worst of all worlds.

Yes, dad-work should either involve a desk and a secretary or a hammer and a helmet. A helmet with a lamp on it. You know, outdoorsy work in freezing cold temperatures that leaves you with rough, grizzled hands and recurring lumbago. That's the respectable way for a father to earn a crust. Either way, dads should come home grumpy and tired and difficult to talk to. They should exude a certain misery that underlines just how much they've sacrificed to put food on their family's table. But a dad who ponces about from one media engagement to the next, coming home at reasonable hours with a skip in his step and a twinkle in his eye? There's something a bit undignified about that, isn't there? It's the sort of thing my grandma would have probably thought of as more than a bit 'queer'.

'We're joined now by journalist Sam Delaney, who's going to give us his sideways glance at the day's newspapers. Welcome to the studio, Sam!'

I frown. I hesitate. I do all the things I know I'm not supposed to do on a live radio station. I open my mouth to speak, but all that comes out is a noise halfway between a cough and a gurgle. It's like the death rattle signalling the sad demise of my broadcasting career.

The presenter, who has been busy staring at her computer screen and hasn't yet bothered to actually look me in the eye, suddenly looks up with an expression of concern.

'Anything, ha ha, anything, erm, caught your eye this morning, Sam?'

'Grrrrhhhuuuh,' I say. It's supposed to mean 'yes', but my larynx doesn't seem to be responding to basic instructions. This aspect of my work shouldn't really be that taxing. A radio station sends a cab to your home. You get in, you go the studio, you shake someone's hand, you walk into the little room, you wait for the presenter to give you the nod and you just start talking. You can say pretty much anything as long as you don't swear, blaspheme, offend the Islamic faith or insult the memory of Princess Diana, Queen of Hearts.

It's hardly a professional skill to rank up there alongside heart surgery or glass-blowing or even hairdressing. But it's something I can do. Occasionally I even do it quite well. But this is my first day back in the saddle after a long and life-changing break. I think I've lost my edge. Most of the talking I've been doing over the past couple of months has been in special cuddly-toy voices. And something tells me that the listening public don't want to hear the Sunday papers reviewed by Barry the Badger. His views would sound even less credible than my own.

'Erm, yes, well. There's some news here,' I eventually manage to splutter while pointing at the front page of a broadsheet.

'What about?' asks the increasingly worried-looking presenter.

'You know, the government have announced a thing about crime, but the other lot have hit back with something else. Hard to say how it will all end up really, isn't it?'

There's a pause.

'OK, that's great. More of Sam's musings coming up after the travel with Laura!'

The sound of beeping horns and clattering trains rumbles in my headphones over a galloping travel news soundtrack. Then the producer's voice drifts above it. 'That was great Sam, thanks,' it says. 'Actually, we're really running out of time, so I think we can let you go now. There's a cab waiting outside for you.'

I thank the host, who doesn't even bother to look up as she says goodbye. I don't blame her. The producer gives me an insincere smile of gratitude as I leave; the eighteen-year-old runner shoots me a look of sympathy. It's a bit humiliating, I suppose. I'm being unceremoniously booted out after just forty seconds back at work. This should have been a nice and easy way to reacclimatise myself to professional life. I made an effort. I even put some proper trousers on and everything. But I flailed about like an amateur. It wasn't as if I just forgot how to speak with fluency or wit. I forgot how to speak altogether. Which, along with stringing the odd nifty sentence together on a keyboard, is one half of my entire skill set down the drain.

My mind may not ever have been as sharp as a razor, but it had its moments. Now it is as blunt and useless as a rusty butter knife. My tongue, once quick and nimble and always ready with a puerile remark or brilliantly idiotic *bon mot*, is now fat and bloated and cumbersome. There is no edge or urgency left inside me. It seems domestic life and fatherhood have sucked it all away and replaced it with a cosy sense of complacent indifference. I haven't felt as content in years. Or as useless.

Even my dad had knuckled down and got a proper job by the time he was my age. And I've always looked on him as some sort of maverick Kerouac figure in comparison to me.

It's not like I have any other career options to fall back on either. I don't have a trade up my sleeve. My 65-year-old neighbour knocked round the other day and asked me to change the cartridge in her Glade Air Freshener. I managed to break it, cut my hand and drop the cup of tea she'd made me all over her carpet. Suffice to say, I'm unlikely to find much work as an odd-job man. Spouting shit on air and in print is pretty much all I've ever known. What else could I possibly do? I did that milk round with Rab but Unigate would never take me back now; he took off suddenly with his uniform and a crate of Ski yoghurts – tainting me by association. It's only a matter of weeks before my daughter comes off the breast and goes on to bottles of uncompetitively priced SMA formula milk. If I don't remember how to earn a living by then, we're all doomed.

As Richard Gere once said in *An Officer and a Gentleman*: 'I've got no place left to go.'

16

PERSPEX

I arrive uncharacteristically early. I have shaved and am wearing a suit and tie. I order a cappuccino, then pick up a copy of *The Times*, neatly fold it and purse my lips thoughtfully as though examining an interesting news story about Darfur. I am acting like a grown-up.

That's because I am here to meet my financial adviser. That's right, my financial bloody adviser. Idiots like me can have them too, you know. I can't pretend I am constantly on the phone telling him to shift assets between various hedge funds or buy kumquats and sell pork bellies. I just bung him a few quid to invest every time I'm feeling flush in order to stop myself from blowing it all on a puppy or some magic beans.

He arrives after five minutes, and I shoot to my feet extending my hand warmly. He settles into the sumptuous leather armchair opposite my own. My suit, this swanky setting, the armchairs and the cappuccinos: it's all a pointless charade really. I suppose I think it will impress him. But what the hell does he care? He's not my bank manager. This isn't a job interview. He works for me. I wouldn't treat my cleaner like this – and that's not me being snobby either. It's just that she's Polish and shy and has a rubbish grasp of the English language, despite having lived here for over two years. The other day I asked her if she enjoyed her summer trip back to Warsaw and she replied, 'Sixteen pounds.' If I took her out for a posh coffee at a fancy West End bar every time I wanted to brief her on the laundry or the dusting, she'd just feel uncomfortable.

But this financial bloke carries a briefcase and chucks about terms like 'tax redemption', 'yield spread premium' and 'self-amortising loan' with casual aplomb. He's serious and intimidating. Something in my subconscious tells me I have to impress him. In reality, I might be better off going for the sympathy vote by arranging to meet him by some swings then turning up in a pair of wee-stained pyjamas and offering him a sip from my plastic bottle of economy cider. At least that way he might leave the meeting feeling a moral responsibility to manage my financial investments with renewed vigour.

As it is, I'm showing him that I'm just about rich enough for him not really to bother about my welfare but not quite rich enough for him to consider me one of his top-class clients who might one day help him retire to a big house made out of jewels in the Caribbean.

I order him a cappuccino. 'Is it as bad as they're all saying?' I ask.

'What?' he says.

'The, erm, what d'you call it? Credit card crunch?'

'The what?' he says angrily.

'I mean the credit crunch. Not credit card. Just credit in general. It's all getting crushed, isn't it?'

There is a silence.

'I suppose you've seen what's been happening in the markets,' he finally says, motioning at my folded copy of *The Times*. I nod thoughtfully, like I was just immersed in a scrupulous analysis of the financial pages before he arrived. Then I shift the paper casually aside, so he won't see that I was actually perusing the TV listings to check what time this afternoon's screening of *The Karate Kid 2* starts on Sky Movies.

'Now's not the time to do anything hasty,' he says. 'The last thing you should do is panic-sell.'

'Sell what?' I think to myself. At the height of its value my investment portfolio would have struggled to finance a trip to Londis to purchase a packet of wine gums and some bin bags.

I have made little progress since my early days as a NatWest Young Saver. Back then I dreamed of one day laying my hands on a sacred porcelain rendition of Sir Nathaniel Westminster. Sir Nathaniel was the piggy bank that NatWest sent you when your savings balance reached a hundred quid. He was an imperious fellow dressed in a three-piece pinstripe suit and red bow-tie, with a pair of half-moon spectacles. Maybe, had my brothers not mugged me out of that money during the ill-fated poker game of 1985, I might have a Sir Nathaniel by now. Perhaps I might have gone beyond Sir Nathaniel and graduated to a giant piggy bank called something like Lord Sebastian Oinkworthy the Third, whom NatWest store in their deepest underground vaults for the real fat cat customers. But, for whatever reason, my finances have pretty much always been a shambles ever since I was wrongly deprived of that winning pot back when I was ten. I think it probably instilled in me an 'easy come, easy go' philosophy which has discouraged me from ever putting much aside for a rainy day.

'I'm afraid your investments are likely to fall in value before they rise,' says the adviser in the same tone of voice that a vet once used to inform me of my dog's pancreatic cancer.

'Oh well,' I say jovially. 'What's nothing take away nothing anyway?'

He doesn't respond.

'That's right: nothing!' I continue.

Still no answer.

'Or is it, in fact, something? Don't two minuses make a plus?'

He ignores me and stirs his coffee with a weary look on his face.

Of course, all I was really hoping to get from him was some advice on scraping together some extra dough. A tax loophole or a benefit scam or something. I've got a kid now: shouldn't that qualify me for some kind of governmental reward scheme? I mean, I voted for Labour. What's the point of putting the pinkos in charge, if you don't get a hand-out when you need one? When we were kids, my mum used to get the family allowance (or 'The Fam', as she called it) once a month. It was a nice little bonus on top of her measly wages, which, on a month when she hadn't been caning the Dorothy Perkins store card too hard, we could spend on little treats like a takeaway or 'a binge'.

'Sod it, I've just got The Fam – let's all have a binge,'

she'd say. We'd cheer with excitement at the prospect of a night in front of the box with a wild array of confectionery, fizzy pop and booze. One of my brothers would be dispatched down the offy to buy my mum a bottle of Martini Extra Dry and a large box of Maltesers. They'd get beers and crisps for themselves, and I'd ordinarily go for some Rolos, a Marathon and a two-litre bottle of R Whites. We were always Labour supporters in our house, but on binge nights I think we may all have said a secret inner thank-you to Mrs Thatcher's government for The Fam and all the wonderful spoils it brought us. 'She may have raped society, sunk the *Belgrano* and stitched them miners up, but she's not all bad,' I'd quietly think as I sank my teeth into the rich caramel centre of another Rolo. Of course, it probably wasn't Thatcher who actually introduced the Fam but at least she hadn't got round to abolishing it yet. Which was nice of her.

My mum worked as a secretary at a Perspex sign company opposite my primary school. She was based in the offices upstairs, but it was down to the basement that I would head once I'd finished my school day and nipped across the road to meet her. It was down where they actually made the signs. I became mates with the staff of West Indian machinists, who would let me watch them at work and occasionally give me a go on the lethal-looking Perspex-cutting contraptions. I loved Perspex. When I was nine years old, it was like a full-blown obsession. Maybe it was all the bright colours it came in; maybe it was the fact it was so flexible and strong; or maybe it was just that it smelt a bit like petrol. Other kids' rooms were full of *Star Wars* figures, Lego or Meccano, but there was a time when mine was filled almost exclusively with Perspex. It was so versatile: I could fight with it. I could use it as a pretend gun, a sword or a dagger. I could get a long, bendy bit, tie a piece of string between each end and fire a shorter, spikier bit from it like a bow and arrow. Also, I could melt it with a Clipper lighter and inhale the toxic fumes. Aesthetically, it lent my room a touch of post-industrial cool, a bit like The Hacienda but with a West Ham bed-spread and a torn-out *Smash Hits* poster of Five Star stuck to the wall.

'A kid like that shouldn't be running around down here,' said Bill, the humourless hunchback supervisor whenever he saw me frolicking amid the dangerous tools and plastics. Of course, he was right. Looking back, I think most of the factory workers were too pissed or stoned at that time of day to monitor me properly. As I slashed and jabbed at an imaginary adversary with my length of green plastic across the factory floor, it was a miracle I didn't at least once trip and cut my own head off in one of the machines. But we didn't appreciate the danger at the time. We thought Bill was just a miserable old bastard who was trying to ruin our fun.

Once, one of the younger workers called Tony got me one of those fake rusty nails from the joke shop that you slip on your finger. We covered it in a generous amount of tomato ketchup, and Tony picked me up and started running around the factory floor like a madman shouting, 'Help! Help! Call an ambulance! The boy's got a nail tru his hand! Jesus Christ! Somebody do something!' I screamed my head off in a brilliantly real portrayal of agony and terror. Within seconds Bill came hobbling round the corner shouting, 'I fucking told you about letting him play down here! You wouldn't listen!'

I screamed some more. Tony stifled his giggles.

'Take me upstairs to where my mum sits,' I whispered out of the side of my mouth. He barged up the stairs still holding me and shouting, 'Get Brenda! Get Brenda! Her boy's mangled his hand!'

In the more refined environs of the upstairs offices all hell broke loose as this giant Jamaican in overalls rampaged about the place clutching a screaming child with blood apparently streaming from his hand. My mum rushed out of her office, grabbed my hand, took one look and said, 'Very funny, you couple of stupid bastards.' She wasn't even being sarcastic. She thought the whole stunt was hilarious. (Mind you, she was an office prankster herself. She used to sneak into the blokes' loos and stretch cling film over the toilet bowls so it was almost invisible. The bosses would go in to take a leak, and all the wee would splash back up all over their trousers.) Anyway, I wasn't allowed back in the factory after that, and Tony got an official warning from Bill. See what I mean? Miserable old bastard.

Another time my mum got an unexpected tax rebate from the Inland Revenue. Once she'd paid off a few outstanding debts, she took me and my brothers up to Wembley Market, each with a roll of notes in our pockets. I bought a fluorescent orange cable-knit jumper, a black bomber jacket and a chunky neck chain in fake silver. I'd actually gone there with the intention of getting a Soda Stream and some records but, during the course of the morning, had developed a strange admiration for the rough-looking blokes who ran the stalls and decided to waste my dough on trying to mimic their dress sense.

In any case, there always seemed to be some way of stumbling on the odd cash injection in times of need when my mum was skint. I was hoping this adviser fellow might scheme up something similar. Times are tough. I couldn't have predicted that the arrival of my first dependant would coincide with a total loss of faith in my own professional capabilities. I haven't managed to complete a decent day's work in weeks. I feel like a cat that's been neutered. My mind is filled with nursery rhymes and shitty nappies and is steadfastly refusing to be cajoled into anything approaching focused, disciplined, work-like thinking. Meanwhile, the baby is due to come off the breast in a matter of weeks, and all that SMA formula milk isn't going to pay for itself.

The crime show I was working on ended in tears, by the way. After my little period at home playing a full-time dad, I just didn't feel ready to go back to the front line of criminality. My first day back on the project was with the drug squad in Reading. A cameraman and myself were to accompany a team of armoured officers on a drug raid on a house being used as a marijuana farm by a Vietnamese gang. Sounds brilliant, right? And it was. The lead officer smashed the door in with a battering ram at 7 o'clock in the morning. As everyone piled into the house, I was in the thick of things, yelping with excitement and trepidation. I anticipated a shoot-out or at least a minor scuffle in which the gang members might try to employ elaborate kung-fu manoeuvres against the cops. But all we found was a timid nineteen-year-old Vietnamese stooge huddled in the corner of the front room amid an impressive forest of skunk weed. They nicked him and threw him in the back of a van. I just stood there taking pictures of the drugs on my mobile and sending them to my mates. Admittedly, it was hardly the sort of journalistic conduct that marks you out for a Pulitzer Prize. My producer encouraged me to confront the prisoner with a hard-nosed line of questioning about the venomous effect his dirty foreign drug-harvesting had on decent British society.

'Give him both barrels,' I was told as I climbed inside the van to confront him. But I just half-heartedly wafted the microphone in his face and said, 'How do you feel, mate?' He tried to answer then started to sob. I found myself giving him an awkward hug and my own eyes unexpectedly welled up with tears. It wasn't what you'd call Paxman-esque.

People had warned me that this would happen once I became a dad. Inexplicable emotion and girlish sentimentality keep washing over me when I least expect it. Maybe it's because fatherhood encourages you to see the world in a broader sense and interpret all the pain and sadness and wrong-doing through the prism of your child's young life. Maybe it's because some tiny part of your heart breaks on the day you see that child come into the world. Or maybe it's because you just turn into a big soppy tart from all that time changing nappies and playing with cuddly badgers and that. Whatever the reason, I just felt too soft and mushy to play the part of a cut-price Roger Cook.

It was just unfortunate timing that my first few months of fatherhood should coincide with a job that entailed long days spent in the company of Yardies, Triads and other assorted ne'er-do-wells in the murkiest quarters of Britain's underworld. My existence became an improbable mix of drug raids and nappies, firearms and blankies, garrotting wires and num-nums.

And, for the uninitiated, 'num-num' is not a new breed of vicious drug criminal from Sri Lanka but baby slang for a dummy. Furthermore, if there are any parenting fascists tut-tutting as they read this, then, no, I don't give my baby a num-num. I just like to use the word because it sounds cute. It's just one of many words and phrases that have found a new appeal since I became a father. 'Snuggle', 'bum-bum', 'nip-nap-noo' and indeed 'booby' are all terms that now spill from my mouth as easily as expletives. Holding a baby in my arms has made me, for some reason, speak in a babyish manner. Which presented the odd communicative faux pas when trying to interact with hard-nosed villains. Things reached their nadir when I accidentally slipped the term 'cheeky-chops' into a chat with a member of the Turkish heroin mafia. You should have seen the look he gave me! A few days later I got the call from my agent: the producers were taking me off the job. The words made it sound like I was a maverick New York cop having his gun and badge taken away because of his cavalier approach to law enforcement. But the truth was almost the complete opposite: I was having my principal source of income removed because fatherhood had turned me into a big soppy idiot.

Things were starting to look bleak. That's why I called the financial adviser.

But what good is he doing me? He's been sitting before me in that armchair speaking in a series of incomprehensible financial terms for almost forty minutes. Eventually he stops and pulls some forms out of his briefcase. Ah, the forms! Those special bits of paper that signal the fact that the meeting's nearly over and everything's going to be OK. All I need to do is sign each of them in three different places and say something like 'That all seems to be in order'. Then he goes away. And I pay for the coffees, which, owing to the needlessly posh location, cost almost as much as a monthly mortgage repayment. I hope this bloke knows what he's doing with my cash.

17

MASTERCHEF

'*Carmella, who the fuck did you think I was when you married me?*' Tony Soprano asks his wife. They are in the pool house. He is wearing a dressing gown. '*You knew my father. You grew up around Dickie Moltisanti and your Uncle Eddie. Where do you get off acting all surprised when there are women on the side? You knew the deal.*'

'*The deal?*' says Carmella in disbelief.

'Yeah, the deal!' I think angrily to myself, glancing at my wife. We are in the bedroom. I am wearing a dressing gown. She is eating a tangerine 'Where do you get off acting all surprised when we end up spending every night watching DVDs in our dressing gowns?'

She's not really surprised. She seems to be enjoying these sedentary evenings in front of the box as much as I am. It could start to get a bit boring and repetitive, I suppose, but I find that pretending in my mind that I am Tony Soprano really helps.

'Stop staring at me like that,' says my wife. I look back at the screen. Tony has just punched a hole in the pool-house wall. I'll probably do that next time we have a row. I start to work out which is the weakest, most flimsy wall in the house.

Not that there's been any rows for a while now. The air of tension and hysteria that prevailed during those first couple of months of sleepless parenthood has finally subsided. Peace and quiet have broken out. Systems have been implemented and routines put in place. The baby's Tet Offensive is over. And it's all thanks to *The Sopranos*. God bless those rotund New Jersey sociopaths.

Our daughter lies sleeping at the end of the bed like a loyal and obedient puppy. The mind games are over. This is how it works every night: we take her into the bedroom, shove a bottle of formula milk in her gob and slap on a *Sopranos* DVD. She is transfixed by it. Maybe it's the tragicomic dialogue or the nuanced meditation on the human condition that permeates every show. Or maybe it's all the fighting and swearing and that. Who knows? Either way, I don't think she could get off to sleep each night without the soothing sounds of Tony pistol-whipping a henchman or Paulie Walnuts hastily digging a grave underneath a flyover. Certainly I'm not about to find out. I've found a night-time routine that works, and I'm sticking to it in every last detail. It's become a superstition – like always wearing the same lucky clothes to the football. The world probably wouldn't cave in if I stopped doing it, but I'd better carry on just in case.

She usually starts to nod off toward the end of the evening's first episode. We leave her lying there on the bed while we sit through another episode, by the end of which she's usually sleeping deeply enough for us to transfer her gently to her cot. After that, if we're both feeling dead saucy and adventurous, we may even watch a third episode. What the hell, we're still relatively young. Who says having kids takes the magic out of a relationship?

If politicians and clergymen really want to find a way of preserving the traditional family unit, then they need look no further than the DVD box set. When your social life has died a slow, painful death, it's cold outside and there's a baby confining you to your house every night of the week, gathering round the telly and watching three hours' worth of high-end American drama is all you've got. It provides an experience that the whole family can share in and bond over. I know it's brought my missus and me closer together. For months we communicated in little more than grunts and sighs. But the other night, as we watched Tony strangle an FBI informant to death with a length of wire, we held each other's hands softly and exchanged a look that seemed to say, 'I'm glad I married you. I'm glad we had our gorgeous daughter. And most of all, I'm glad we invested in seasons 4, 5 and 6 in the HMV sale, because I don't think life can get any better than this.'

Everyone's at it. And it's not just *The Sopranos* either. *The Wire*, *The West Wing*, *Deadwood*: these are the shows that are saving a whole generation of kids from growing up in broken homes. Why would dad stay at the pub for one more drink with the girl from bought ledger when he could be at home, snuggled up with the woman he loves, watching Larry David getting himself embroiled in another calamitous predicament? And how could she ever get bored with a man with whom she's sat through every last episode of *Nip Tuck*? She couldn't. That kind of shared experience runs too deep. It entwines your souls.

No wonder our parents split up. The best they had back in the '70s was *The Sweeney*. And when an episode of that ended, you had to wait an entire week to see what happened next. The frustration must have driven them mad.

Yep, DVDs have made staying in every night of the week actually seem like fun. And somehow more glamorous and cerebral than just sitting there slack-jawed in front of normal, rubbishy, British TV. Soap operas that make you so sick with sadness you feel like ringing up your mum and telling her you need a cuddle; sitcoms so mirthless you'd get more laughs out of contracting the Ebola virus on holiday. TV makes you feel old and fat and bored and pointless. DVD box sets make you feel cool, clever and sexy. Besides, you haven't got the energy to do much else. Parenthood seems to instil in you a unique form of deep-impact fatigue that, older dads tell me, never goes away. There's no light at the end of the tunnel. You've got a life sentence of listlessness. When the day is over and the baby is asleep, you don't have the energy to do anything worthwhile like build a matchstick *Cutty Sark* or play Guess Who? with your partner. It takes pretty much all you've got left just to shove that silver disc in the DVD player and press 'play'.

We did try and go out together a few Fridays ago. My father-in-law was visiting from Hungary, so he agreed to baby-sit. My wife put on a dress, and I even wore a pair of leather shoes with laces. It was as though we were Richard Burton and Elizabeth Taylor on their way to the 1963 Academy Awards ceremony. Only we were just nipping out to the local cinema for the 6.30 showing of *American Gangster*, starring Denzel Washington. We were just too nervous to do anything more daring. What if the baby woke up and started to cry? What if the house exploded? What if she got hungry and Hungarian granddad started feeding her raw onions in pig fat or pickled fish guts or whatever the hell it is they eat over there? No, it was best we made this a speed date and got back to the house before anyone died.

'Seems a bit of a shame to not . . . you know . . . get a little bit out of it. Seeing as it's the first time we've been out in ages,' my wife ventured as we hurried out the front door.

'What? Are you mental? There's not time for that!' I said in disgust. 'If you want, I'll get you a can of gin and tonic and you can drink it on the bus.'

She ignored me and doubled back up the stairs. I stared at my watch frantically. What was she doing up there? I started calculating that we might actually have to sacrifice watching the last hour or so of *American Gangster* if we were to make it back in reasonable time. It wouldn't matter too much. I mean, the last hour of most films is usually just padding, isn't it?

'Right, let's go,' said my wife, skipping back down the stairs and out the front door with an unusual amount of bonhomie.

'What did you go upstairs for?' I asked once the door had shut behind us.

'This!' she announced, producing a polythene bag of weed from her pocket.

Nothing confirms that you're approaching middle age quite like a bag of stale weed kept in a box on the mantelpiece, does it?

Still, she loves smoking that stuff. And, what with trying to get pregnant, then being pregnant, then breast-feeding, she hasn't been able to touch it for nearly two years. As she sat on the back seat of the bus rolling a spliff, her eyes twinkled with a look that said, 'It's good to see you again, old friend!' I felt happy for her.

Personally, I hate the stuff. It brings on my epilepsy something rotten. When I was seventeen, I walked into an Amsterdam coffee shop with four mates and, trying to act the big man, asked the owner what the strongest gear they had was. He told me it was a special type of hashish called Temple Balls. I boldly slapped my guilders on the counter and told him to serve me up a big fat lump. It was 10 a.m. One of us rolled the biggest, dirtiest spliff I'd ever seen in my life, crammed full of my hash plus the assortment of toxic weeds the others had bought. I had a couple of tokes and immediately started to feel peculiar. But we had a busy itinerary of smoking lined up for the day, and there was no time to hang around. Everyone wanted to go and tick the next coffee shop off the list. As I stood up at the table to follow my mates out of the door, my vision suddenly went blank. All I could see was blackness. I remember frantically waving my own hands in front of my face, to no avail. My last words were 'Hold up, lads!' and a split second later I was on the floor, flapping about like a dying fish. The eyewitness reports weren't pretty: I kicked chairs and tables, I foamed at the mouth and, of course, I pissed my pants. Two of my friends tried to hold me down, but I clawed at their faces and ripped out handfuls of their hair. When I came to, covered in sweat and urine, the first thing I saw was a group of petrified adolescent Germans huddled in the corner with a look of sheer terror on their faces. The poor stoned bastards were probably paranoid enough without some English dingbat performing an incontinent break-dance routine by their feet. The coffee shop proprietor came over and handed me a cup of water.

'Sorry about the mess, mate,' I said croakily.

'Hey, no worriesh!' he smiled. 'Temple Ballsh getsh them every time!'

'Do what?'

'Hey, when five English guysh come in and one of them ordersh a bag of that shtuff, I know for sure only four of them are walking out on two legsh!'

Then he started to laugh. Glad he found it funny, the blood-sucking, drug-pushing Dutch bastard.

Once I got back to England, I started to see a neurologist. He ran a load of tests and brain scans and eventually concluded that my epilepsy was reactive. I was unlikely just to have a fit out of the blue while walking along the street. I had to stimulate it in some way by making myself pass out.

'So what are you trying to say?' I asked him.

'Well, for starters, I'd suggest you never go near another marijuana cigarette again,' said the doc. Well, he would say that, wouldn't he?

Foolhardy and idiotic as I was, I ignored his advice and, as a result, was plagued by similar undignified episodes throughout my late teens and early twenties. The worst was probably the morning I woke up on the fifteenth floor of a hospital twenty miles from home with stitches in my head, blood on my face and wires stuck all over my chest.

I looked around the room and saw about half a dozen elderly men attached to machines lying all around me.

'Where am I?' I asked.

'Cardiac ward, son,' piped up one of the codgers with a slightly irritating smirk.

'Cardiac ward? Which hospital?'

'Kingston,' he replied.

Kingston? What was I doing in Kingston? I didn't even know where Kingston was. I still don't.

'Shit. What happened?' I muttered.

'Well, by the looks of you, you've lost a fight and had a heart attack!' he chuckled. The others joined in. If I'd had the energy, I would have got up and switched their machines off.

I rang my eldest brother.

'You'd better come and get me.'

'Where are you?'

'Kingston Hospital.'

'Why?'

'I've lost a fight and had a heart attack.'

'Oh. Where's Kingston Hospital?'

'I've no idea. Gotta go, there's a doctor coming.'

I put the phone down and scampered up to the doctor with my bumless gown blowing all around me. 'What the fuck?' was all I could say.

According to what they'd been able to piece together from the people who accompanied me in the ambulance, I had been to a football match, got a bit tipsy, travelled across town with some mates, smoked a few moody spliffs, fallen over in a driveway, cut my head on a wall, had a series of seizures and been ferried to the only hospital within a 10-mile radius to have a spare bed on a Saturday night. It just so happened that that spare bed was in the cardiac ward at Kingston. I was relieved. I felt like going up to that old codger who'd laughed at me and saying, 'Guess what? I haven't had a heart attack after all! And you have! IN YOUR FACE GRANDAD!'

Anyway, it wasn't any of those incidents that eventually made me give up smoking gear. It was just the sudden realisation, when I was about twenty-five, that I really didn't like it. I don't think I ever did. It made me feel slow-witted, tired, nauseous and really, really nervous. Nervous about having another fit. Nervous about the other people in the room not liking me. Nervous about how I was going to get home. Nervous that someone might be hiding under the bed. Nervous about North Korea. Just nervous about whatever happened to cross my mind, really. I'd only been smoking it all those years because that was what everyone else around me did. And I didn't have much else on: when your days are filled with nothing but video games, *Home and Away* and Penguin biscuits, then smoking something that induces anxiety and paranoia can actually seem like an amusing distraction. But not when you've got a job or any other sort of preoccupation that requires you to converse with other adults or walk near busy traffic.

We were walking near some busy traffic towards the cinema when my wife offered me the spliff. She knows I don't touch the stuff but still makes the gesture out of habit.

'Fuck it,' I thought. 'We're out on the town! Just like when we were students! It's like the mid-'90s all over again! Come on everyone, let's get battered and dance to

Oasis! Later on we can watch *Trainspotting*! Woo hoo! Girl Power!'

I took two tokes, went a bit dizzy and, just as we were walking into the foyer to collect our tickets, announced that I wanted to go home. Apparently, *American Gangster* was pretty average anyway.

Who needs going out when staying in is so brilliant anyway? The secret to true domestic happiness, I have discovered, is just to give in to it. Buy yourself some loose-fitting cotton trousers with an elasticated waist and embrace the glories of the quiet life. The beauty of it is that my wife can't possibly lose respect for me when she's complicit in the whole thing. Or so I thought.

'I'm going out on Saturday night,' she casually mentions one night during *Masterchef*. (Some British TV shows are OK to watch – specifically the ones designed to reassure you that the humdrum mechanics of domestic life are some kind of exhilarating art form. It helps cultivate a state of false consciousness among the stay-at-home parenting community that rustling up a bit of dinner is a sexy and glamorous experience. Even if, like me, all you usually do is heat up a couple of fish fingers and slap them between two end-slices of Hovis with a bit of ketchup.)

'You're going out? Where? Who with? Is this some sort of joke?' I blurt.

'No. I'm going out with the girls for a few drinks. It won't be a late one.'

Rejection. Hurt. Betrayal. Confusion. I give her a stare that expresses all of these emotions plus some brand new, as yet unnamed ones that I didn't even know I was capable of feeling.

'So, you're breaking ranks, are you?' I say, shaking my head in lament.

'From what?'

'From DVD club! I thought things were going so well!'

'Eh? What difference does it make to you? You can still watch DVDs.'

'No I can't! If I watch any new episodes, you'll be behind! We won't be able to watch them together any more. The system will break! Don't break the system!'

She thinks about this. She knows I've got a point.

'Can't you just watch some episodes and not tell me that you've watched them. Then just sit through them again until I've caught up?'

I am alarmed and appalled by this suggestion.

'No, I most certainly cannot! I will not subvert the system like that. And anyway, you'll be able to tell I've already seen them and get irritated when I'm not as into them as you are.'

'Well, whatever, I'm going out, so you'll have to just find something else to do on Saturday night.'

'I will!' I say petulantly. 'Maybe I'll go out with the boys. And get drunk. And sing songs and . . . that.'

'No. You'll be here, looking after the baby.'

Oh yeah, the baby. Just me and her, left to our own devices. It could be interesting. I feel emboldened by the responsibility that's suddenly been handed to me.

Also, I'm quite glad that my wife is getting to go out. There's a part of me that's been worrying that she might get bored of this cosy life of ours and end up killing herself or cuckolding me with a gardener or a fireman or, worse, a slightly more successful voice-over artist. Then again, I also worry that once she's back out on the town, living a normal, decent, socially interactive life, I will strike her as even more stupid and slothful than I do already. All I can hope is that she comes home so paralytic that she can't even see me sprawled out on the sofa in my tracksuit and slippers covered in Wotsit crumbs. Then wake up with such a bad hangover the next morning that she vows never to go out again. I'll probably be welcoming her back into DVD club with open arms by Sunday night at the latest.

18

BED

I can't believe she's going through with this. Look at her with her make-up and her clothes and her perfume. Putting on her ear-rings. Looking in her mirror. What's she trying to prove? That's she's a better person than me, just because she smells nice and looks nice and generally treats herself with self-respect? Well, she can keep her self-respect. And her dignity. Let her run into the arms of the outside world with its pubs and people and fun and shapes and colours. I'm happy here with my glass of Ribena, my baby and my curiously engaging episode of *In The Night Garden*.

'There's two bottles of formula milk in the fridge,' she says. 'One for bedtime and one in case she wakes up.'

'Hrghuugh,' I say indifferently.

'And she's due a bath.'

'Nnnghn,' I nod.

'And if her gums start to play up, the Calpol is on the shelf in her room.'

'Calpol,' I say perking up. 'Now there's a delicious medicine.'

She glances at the TV screen, then at the baby, then at me.

'Don't watch telly right up until bedtime, will you? She's got that new book you could read her.'

She has now stood in front of the telly in order to command my attention. I lean sideways to see round her. The baby starts to whine half-heartedly.

'Are you listening?' she asks.

'Yes I am listening,' I say. 'Book, bath, bottle, bed. Fun to say, fun to do! Don't worry about us. Go out and have a good time.'

She starts to leave.

'Oh, just one last thing,' I say, just like Colombo.

'What?'

'I was thinking of taking a crap later and I'm not quite sure how to go about wiping my arse afterwards. Could you do me a little diagram?'

She kisses the baby and struts out into her precious, outdoor world.

We go back to *In The Night Garden*. The dim-witted, sponge-like characters tit about in their brightly coloured, hypnotic netherworld. The plot is unfathomable. And yet it's still so compelling. The baby is spellbound. I am too: maybe it's the music; maybe it's the funny gobbledygook they talk. Or maybe it's the gentle, soothing tones of the Derek Jacobi voice-over. Now there's a bloke who knows how to talk out loud. I'd make a real hash out of this: every time I talk it comes out too noisy and squawky and offensive. Fine for the moronic 'urban' masses but terrifying for kids. Even my own daughter, with her tiny ears and rubbish baby brain, cringes when I try to communicate with her verbally. But who needs words when we've got *In The Night Garden*? Somehow, the devilish masterminds behind this show have managed to tap into the fledgling psyche of children who are still too young even to understand their own names. It's sinister in a way, but I'm not complaining. She seems to like the fact that I'm as engaged in it as she is. Every now and again she looks up at my face to check I'm still watching, then smiles, snuggles up and grips my finger in her tiny hand. Then I well up a tiny bit. This show's almost as good as *The Sopranos*.

I'll tell you what: it's better than any of the crap they served up when I was a kid. *The Moomins*, *Willo the Wisp*, *Ivor the Engine*, *Chockablock*: what a load of dreary, depressing old toss. Conceived and executed by a load of stinking old hippies who'd taken too much acid in the '60s and thought it was a good idea to impose their 'far out' ideas on a generation of kids by means of crappy, cheapo animation. Oh, I'd watch it: what choice did I have? But I didn't enjoy it. It made me sad. And don't talk to me about *Bagpuss*. It was a load of rubbishly animated, meaningless bullshit that people who grew up in the '70s and '80s now think is ironic and clever to harp on about. Professor Yaffle: what a pompous know-it-all. If he came round my way shouting the odds, I'd set fire to the stupid wooden fucker.

The programme finishes. The baby looks at me. I look at the Nintendo Wii. 'Would now be an appropriate time for me to have a quick session on Super Mario Kart?' I ask myself. 'Maybe she's ready to join in on a two-player time trial? It could be fun. And educational.'

I switch on the console, start up the game and hand her a controller. She starts to lick it like a Cornetto. The race starts. I'm off to a flyer. She seems content enough. Then

'Bump!' She falls over backwards and smacks her head on the floorboards. I suppose the ability to sit upright for more than ten seconds at a time is a prerequisite for this sort of thing. She's rubbish at video games.

'So, what shall we do now?' I ask her once she's stopped crying. My wife had made mention of a book, but I'm not in the mood. She's got years of enforced reading at school ahead of her – the last thing she needs is me imposing a load of boring books on her prematurely. Besides, it's Saturday night and Mum's out. 'Let's go wild! Raid the Malibu! Order an extra-large meat-free pizza delivery and don't bother with a side salad! Invite some older kids round and try to skin up using oregano and dried banana skins!' She blinks back at me, with a distinct lack of enthusiasm.

I rummage through the cupboard and find her toy *du jour*: the electro drum. Her face lights up at the first glimpse of it. Personally, I find it a monotonous and rudimentary device, especially in comparison to the Wii. You whack it, it bleeps. You whack it again, it bleeps again. It's like R2-D2 without the mechanical expertise, computer hacking abilities or cheeky banter. Still, there's a certain thrill to be had from just watching the baby's excitable responses to it, I suppose. She likes it even more when I join in. Whack! Bleep. Whack! Bleep. Whack, whack, whack! Bleepety bleep blop. Whack, tap, whack, whack, kerpow!

Wait a minute! What's this? My random sequence of freestyle jazz whacking seems to have unlocked the hidden abilities of the electro drum! Suddenly, it's launched into a high-octane calypso freakdown. I sweep the baby up in my arms and we dance into the kitchen. I shuffle soulfully across the tiles, nimbly tiptoeing between the cat's litter tray and biscuit bowl. She whoops with glee, shimmies her shoulders, then, lost in all the excitement, tries to shove her index finger into my eye. It feels like being at Studio 54. Or at least a really good Billy Ocean concert. It's a special moment. And then she starts to giggle. It starts as a smirk, turns into a titter and suddenly she's laughing out loud like a big, silly idiot. It may sound a bit corny, but there really is nothing quite as brilliant and fulfilling as making her laugh. Not just because it sounds nice. And not just because it proves that you're beginning to bond and communicate in some meaningful way. Mainly, it's a competitive thing. My wife and I are locked in a constant, niggling contest to see who can elicit the most laughter out of our child. And while she's out neglecting her parental duties and having a so-called 'good time', I've stolen a march on her.

This battle has been intensifying with each passing week. Yesterday I was locked away in the front room trying to work when the captivating sound of her giggles drifted under the crack in the door and wafted round my head like Bisto fumes.

'What's going on in there?' I called out, dead jealous of all the merriment. There was a pause.

'Nothing,' my wife said, all shifty.

We lust after baby laughter like desperate junkies, trying ever more ludicrous ways to elicit the tiniest bit of precious giggling from her tiny larynx. She's no easy audience either. Standard tactics like the raspberry on the tummy don't wash with her. Games of peek-a-boo are an insult – she sighs and gives me her 'Try again, you tiresome little prick' look. Her sneering attitude makes the occasional chuckle seem even more precious. Whenever her little face opens up into beaming frivolity, I go dizzy with euphoria.

And if laughter is the commodity, then jokes are the currency. I covet them with a raging obsession.

'You're making her laugh!' I called out to my wife in an accusatory tone. 'I heard you! How did you do it? Was it the thing with her toes? Was it the monkey face? TELL ME, DAMN YOU!'

But she didn't tell me, just as I wouldn't tell her if the tables were turned. Like I say, this pursuit of laughter is turning ugly. It's only a matter of time before one of us dresses up as a clown and starts careering round the front room on a unicycle. And no one will be laughing then, will they?

After all the laughter and electro drumming she's in no mood for bed. I stick her in the bath, which she immediately pisses into, causing further hysteria.

We're on the bed in the established manner: me in my dressing gown, her in her jim-jams. She has a bottle in her gob and, it being Saturday night and everything, I am drinking a can of Kronenbourg. I can see her eyes twitching around suspiciously as she drinks her milk. She knows something's not quite right. She misses *The Sopranos*.

'*Family Fortunes*?' she seems to be saying as I flick through the channels. '*Family fucking Fortunes*? Are you having a laugh or what?'

I keep flicking. *Midsomer Murders*, *The National Lottery*, the news?

'Come off it, Dad,' her eyes tell me. 'This is just insulting.'

'But *CBeebies* finishes at seven! What am I supposed to do? I can't mess with the system!' I tell her, pointlessly.

She looks at me with what I can only interpret as disgust.

Then I stumble on the rugby. Apparently it's the world cup final. Just an excuse for public school boys to feel each other up, if you ask me, but to my surprise she actually seems to like it. She's snuggled back up and clutched my finger in that tear-inducing way again.

'What the hell,' I think to myself. 'It's a big event, and England are playing. No one need ever know that I've watched it. Let's give it a go.'

I crack open another lukewarm can from the four-pack that's sat beside the bed.

By the time she's finished the bottle, the game seems to be reaching its conclusion. I've not really managed to make much sense of it, but England are definitely losing. She's straining to keep her eyelids open, clearly more engrossed in the match than I am. Eventually she gives in and drifts off.

'I'll give it till full time, then I'll stick her in the cot,' I think to myself.

But by full time I've fallen asleep too. I wake up in a fug about an hour and a half later. She is lying on my chest, face down, dribbling on to my throat. The remote has got jammed under my arse and the telly screen has gone all fuzzy. I flick back to BBC 1, where *Match of the Day* is starting. The baby doesn't flinch. She's deep under. Really I should put her in the cot, but we're too cosy like this. I wonder how my wife could possibly be having a better time than me right now. I've propped myself up on a pillow, the baby is all warm on top of me like a living, breathing electric blanket and the football's just started.

By the way, I understand that this whole scenario sounds like a lamentable and contrived depiction of what some doofus might perceive to be a laddish fantasy, but what can I tell you? I like European cinema with subtitles, I eat salad most days, I moisturise, I exercise, I've even been known to read a bit of poetry in my time. I'm as modern as the next poncey metrosexual dickhead. But sometimes you can forget how enjoyable the most obvious and clichéd things can be. It's like 'Don't You Want Me', by The Human League. It's become such a staple at weddings and naff office parties that you start to think it's just some sort of stupid novelty track. You relegate it in your brain to the status of 'I'm Too Sexy' by Right Said Fred or 'Mr Blobby' or something. But then, one day, when you've managed to avoid hearing it for about five years and you're driving along in the car on your own in an above-average mood, that magnificent, seductive, twinkling synth intro kicks in and you think to yourself: 'I LOVE this song. What is it again? Shit! It's "Don't You Want Me"! "Don't You Want Me" is in fact one of my all-time favourite songs! It's only artificial cultural connotations that have somehow stigmatised it and altered my perceptions of what is actually the quintessential British pop classic. Damn those artificial cultural connotations. Always getting in the way of my fun.'

That's what having a beer in front of the football feels like. You realise that before it became a cliché it was actually really good. In fact, it became a cliché because it was so good.

Also, I am aware that boshing four cans of strongish continental lager while in charge of an infant is probably not in the parenting handbook or anything. But she's pretty much immobile, so she can't really escape my clutches and start jamming her fingers in electric sockets, no matter how drunk I get. Plus, my mild tipsiness has ushered a nice, relaxed atmosphere into the house this evening. That's why she's drifted off so peacefully. She's very receptive to the prevailing vibe. And anyway, it's not like I'm legless and have been knocking back chasers or anything. I may be merry, but I am in control.

I hear a key in the door. This should be interesting. Just wait till she sees how well things have gone in her absence. So much for going out being the new staying in. Staying in is the new staying in! Reclining comfortably on the bed, cushioned by a gigantic maternity pillow, I smile smugly.

'I am a natural father', I think to myself for the first time. I look out of the bedroom window, see the comforting orange light of the street lamp reflecting in the glass and inhale that comforting, autumnal whiff of burning leaves. Everything is right with the world. Only, those burning leaves don't smell too healthy. In fact, they smell more like . . . what is it? Burning hair? Where exactly is it coming from?

'Fuck!' exclaims my wife as she enters the room. 'The bed's on fire, the bed's on fire! You're burning the fucking baby, you fuckwit!'

I chuckle condescendingly and briefly protest.

'I'm not burning anythi . . .' But then I glance to my left and realise she is quite right. The corner of the maternity pillow has caught fire on the wall-mounted bedside lamp.

My wife wrenches the baby from my grasp. As I frantically beat down the flames, I surreptitiously sweep the empty beer cans under the bed with my foot so she won't see them.

Later, once the baby's safely asleep in her cot and we've had a chance to take stock, we have a full and frank discussion about what happened. Or rather I slouch, head in hands, bemoaning my own pathetic failings as a father and human being.

'I hate myself,' I say for about the fortieth time in the past hour.

'Shit happens,' shrugs my wife.

'Not that kind of shit. We could have died,' I insist, shaking my head.

'It wasn't that bad!' she says. It's nice of her to comfort me. But I'm not sure anyone can help me now. I thought I might not have what it takes to be a dad, and now I know I was right. I haven't quite toasted the baby's hand in a sandwich-maker, but I wasn't far off. What scant self-respect I ever possessed has dissolved into a sorry puddle of self-loathing.

'Did you have a nice time, at least?' I snivel.

'Yes I did,' she says. 'It was a nice change, you should try it.'

'What?' I say, raising my head slowly. 'Going . . . out?'

'I think it'd do you good,' she smiles.

'You just want me away from the baby for a while, don't you? You think I'm a liability, is that it?'

'No. It's not that. It's just . . .'

'Yes?'

'Well, you have been acting a bit . . . mental lately.'

'Oh.'

'You may need to go out. Do the things you used to do. See your mates. Remind yourself that you're a good bloke.'

'How is seeing my mates going to remind me that I'm a good bloke? All my mates call me a wanker,' I blub.

'They don't mean it. They're just being funny,' she smiles.

'Yeah, they are funny, aren't they?' I say, allowing a tiny grin to bleed slowly across my mournful face. I picture my mates standing round in the pub, listening to the story of me accidentally burning the bed, slapping me on the back and calling me a wanker. 'Really funny,' I reiterate.

'Right then, next Saturday is your day,' my wife insists. 'And we shall never speak of this shameful incident ever again.'

19

DRUGS

'Wanker.'

'Wanker.'

'Dickhead.'

'Wanker.'

'Mug.'

I have just told my mates about setting the bed on fire. It's not a bad response, I suppose. I didn't exactly expect a round of applause. But I had thought they might at least chuckle a bit while they insulted me. Maybe even slap me on the back, reassure me that they've all made similar mistakes in the past and tell me not to be so hard on myself. But they don't. They just shake their heads in judgemental disgust and carry on calling me names for a few more minutes. This isn't helping me to feel better about myself at all.

These are the men with whom I've been going to football for the past seventeen years. We have travelled the UK and beyond together to watch our team lose. We have drunk together, we have laughed together and we have fallen over together. In case you're wondering, no, we have never cried together – we're not that bloody close. But we've shared some of life's most poignant, coming-of-age moments. We have grown up in each other's idiotic company. These are my mates. Yes, they may be the sort of mates who will call you a wanker, who will mock everything you say and do, who will put sweet wrappers and fag-ends in your mouth when you fall asleep on the train, who will steal your shoes and throw them in a river and who will sometimes question the very point of your existence. But they are mates nonetheless. Mates who, when push comes to shove, would be there for you when you really needed them. As long as they weren't busy with other, more important stuff.

Among them is one of my brothers. He was the one who got me into all this in the first place. When I was a kid, each of my three older brothers supported a different London team. Each of them tried to lobby and harangue me into following their respective sides. It was my middle brother who proved successful. He was the same one who would later 'teach' me boxing and pull a knife on Rab the milkman. Suffice to say, he had always been the one with the most persuasive personality. So I ended up going to West Ham like him.

I look at him. He's the only one yet to pass comment on the bed incident. He's keeping his counsel. I should imagine he's feeling a bit sorry for me. Protective even. He'll probably say something to make me feel a bit better in a minute. He drains his drink and fixes me with fiery eyes full of . . . what is it? Hate? No, it's gentler than that. Disappointment? No, not that either. Disdain. That's the word for it.

'Silly bastard,' he says. At least he has the decency to fix me in the eye sincerely when he says it. The others earnestly nod in agreement. They all turn their backs and talk among themselves.

We are in a pub in a village somewhere in Berkshire. We are on our way to watch West Ham play at Reading. Whenever we leave London, we like to get off the train a few stops before our final destination, pick out a secluded pub and get a bit drunk before heading off to the game. It's a routine, a tradition, a method of having fun. I can't remember why it's fun. Written down here in black and white, it doesn't sound like fun at all. But then, the ins and outs of what objectively constitutes a fun experience are neither here nor there. My brain has been trained for many years to categorise these cold, uncomfortable, inebriated afternoons as 'fun experiences', and who am I to argue with my own brain? This is just what I do at the weekend.

At least, it's what I used to do. Right now, I am feeling badly out of practice. Frankly, I'm struggling to keep up, like a little kitten thrown into a lion's den. Although I wouldn't really say this lot are like lions – more like a collection of rancid strays. The point is, I've known them most of my life, but after my leave of absence they seem like strangers to me now. They speak so quickly; their language is so lewd and coarse; they drink, they smoke and they pull these scary faces while they talk. It's all so confusing. Can't we all just sit down and have some quiet time for five minutes? I need a wee. I feel sick. I can't hear what any of them are saying. I don't think I've had a conversation with more than one adult at a time for about six months. I have to keep reminding myself not to lapse into my Barry Badger voice. I wonder how my brother would react if I asked him for a cuddle.

'I knew you weren't cut out for fatherhood,' snarls one of the throng.

'Why not?' I respond, all stuttery and high-pitched.

'Coz you barely know how to wipe your own arse, let alone someone else's. Setting fire to a baby? That's a bit off really, isn't it? Let's be honest – it's borderline noncing.'

I pause. I croak. I try to think of an appropriate comeback.

'Yeah, well, at least I'm not . . . a bloody . . . gay,' is the best I can muster.

'What?'

'That's what you are,' I say with a fake chuckle, hoping some of the others will join in with my rubbishy line of mockery. 'You're like a big gay!'

I point a limp, accusatory finger at him to emphasise my point. It doesn't matter. Everyone's shaking their heads and looking at me pitifully. They go back to talking among themselves.

I used to be good at this. I could take the banter and dish it back out. Now all I can come up with is a mumbled chunk of embarrassing playground homophobia that even a real-life playground homophobe would probably consider too witless and ineloquent to employ.

I have let my mates down, the gay community down and, most of all, myself down. You know you've hit rock bottom when you struggle to match the beer-sodden repartee of a bar load of West Ham fans. I mean, this isn't exactly *the Oxford Union Debating Society*. All you really have to do is swear loudly and with venom and they'll accept you as one of their own. But I haven't had what you might call a right proper swear-up in ages. At best, I've been limited to a bit of light 'domestic swearing' around the house. You know, nothing major, just the odd angry exclamation after stubbing a toe on the coffee table or injuring a knuckle on the cheese-grater. The other day I shouted 'Fuck you!' at our gas-fuelled open fire after singeing my eyebrows while lighting it. It felt briefly liberating until I heard my wife shouting 'Stop swearing at the fire' from upstairs. Stupid baby monitor.

It's not just the dialogue I'm struggling to keep up with either. It's the drinking too. The speed with which they're sinking pints is preposterous. They're making them disappear like magicians. I'm having trouble getting the first down my throat. It's freezing outside, and the cold, fizzy lager feels like it's solidified into a gigantic iceberg halfway down my gullet, forming a ballast against any more liquid entering the body. Inside my lungs lurks a painful burp that can't be expended and which is causing a stabbing sensation to spread across my entire chest. Perhaps I'm having a heart attack? Best not to mention it: they'll only take the piss. I secretly spill half of my remaining pint into a pot plant and hope no one notices.

I thought drinking less would be a natural benefit of fatherhood. But I was wrong. All I have done is spread my boozing out more thinly across the week. Whereas I used to avoid drink all week long and binge at weekends, I now drink small amounts on a daily basis. I find a can of Foster's at about half-seven every night – just after I've got home from work, bathed the baby, put her to bed, done a bit of housework, caught up on some e-mails and contemplated the fact that all of this will start over again at about 6 o'clock the next morning – helps stave off the nagging suspicion that I may be losing the will to live.

But binge-drinking is out of the question. It's hard enough waking up at 4 a.m. to wipe shit off another human being's arse at the best of times. But with a pounding headache, a mouth like Chernobyl and a stomach full of acid and regret, it's simply unthinkable. So I have now learned to stop drinking after a maximum of two alcoholic units per night.

Now, after a long spell on the sidelines, I have been unceremoniously thrust back on to the front line of binge-drinking. It's been a terrifying, high-speed booze assault from the moment I arrived at Paddington Station at 10 o'clock this morning and found them guzzling cans from their Thresher's carrier bags. There is no mercy, no retreat and no surrender in this sort of drinking environment. I want to go home.

'Another pint?' someone asks.

'Erm, I might just have a ha . . .'

But it's too late. They have handed me a large, gassy glass of freezing-cold continental lager and a small glass of unsolicited whisky to go with it. And they are watching me. They smell blood. They sense my powers have been weakened. But they will not see me fail today. I know how to do this. Pathetic, pointless, macho drinking habits were what I was brought up with. Now is the time for me to call upon all that experience and show them what I'm made of. I slam the whisky down my throat with a wince. I immediately bring the beer to my lips and begin to guzzle hungrily, my eyes shut and my toes secretly curled inside my shoes. There, that showed them.

'Sam, Sam, wake up you bell-end.'

I can feel a hand on my shoulder. Where am I? I open my eyes and see a shiny, wet, *faux* mahogany table-top staring back at me. I can smell stale fag ash and chip fat. I look up. My friends are standing around looking quizzical. They are shaking their heads again.

'What happened? Did I have a fit?' I ask.

'No.'

'Did one of you knock me out?'

'No. You fell asleep, you twat.'

'Shit. How long was I out for?'

'I dunno. Forty seconds.'

I try to shake the fuzziness from my head.

'Look, I didn't get much sleep last night. The baby's teething and . . .'

I look at their stupid faces and detect a softening of attitude. A few of this lot are dads themselves. They know what it's like.

'Mate, you'll get used to it,' someone says, putting an arm round me.

'I remember the first time I went to football after my first was born,' says another, wistfully. 'Arsenal away, it was. Spewed all over a steward's shoes. Cunt threw me out.'

There's a silence as everyone contemplates this moving anecdote.

Eventually Frank comes over and puts an arm round me. He's the youngest of the group and always has a grin on his face and an ill-thought-out plan for misadventure hovering perilously on his lips. He starts leading me towards the pub's back door.

'Come on, I'll sort you right out,' he says.

He leads me into the beer garden and towards a concrete out-house.

'Where are we going?' I ask.

'The kitchens,' he smiles.

'What for?'

'To see the chef.'

'Are you buying me a bacon sandwich?'

'No. Even better. I'm going to buy you some lovely drugs.'

'What? No, I don't want any lovely drugs. Thanks all the same.'

'How else are you going to wake up?' he asks incredulously.

'Trust me, they won't make me wake up. They'll make me go all epileptic. Don't make me take the lovely drugs, Frank.'

But there's no stopping him. I am being forced towards the kitchen door.

'How are we going to get drugs in here?' I ask.

He looks incredulous again, as though I'm the one being stupid.

'Every village pub chef in Britain sells coke on the side,' he explains. 'Didn't you know that?'

'No. I did not know that,' I say.

'Trust me, I used to live in a village. Think about it: how else are they making their money?' he asks almost rhetorically.

Before I have a chance to make sense of the question, we are inside the kitchen. There is a fat man in his forties microwaving a plastic jug full of baked beans. There is also a spotty-faced teenager fetching something from the freezer and a rotund, smiley-faced waitress arranging things on a tray. Their heads turn, and they regard the pair of us with sullen indifference. I blink and try to look apologetic. Frank grins confidently and sways around a bit in the doorway.

'Hello pal,' he barks at the chef, who, to my untrained eye, makes for an unlikely-looking drug-dealer. 'We're looking for Charlie.'

The chef exchanges a confused glance with his two underlings, then looks back at us and says in a timid, bumpkinish voice:

'I beg your pardon?'

'You know, a bit of gear?' Frank elaborates with a wink.

Again, the kitchen staff just gawp at us in bafflement.

'Look, mate,' says Frank, a hint of exasperation creeping into his voice, 'all we're looking for is a bit of chop, right?'

Even I'm losing track of the euphemisms now. I don't like this. It doesn't feel like a dad thing to be doing on a Saturday afternoon. I should really be at Homebase buying Rawlplugs.

'I'm sorry, but I really don't know what you mean,' says the chef politely.

'SNIFF!' shouts Frank, the beer and frustration getting to him. 'WE'RE LOOKING FOR SNIFF!'

'Steph?' says the chef. 'Sorry mate, Steph doesn't work here any more. She got a job at the Bell and Crown up the road, you'll have to go up there I'm afraid.'

Frank is furious. 'Come on, we're going,' he says, tugging me by the arm and stomping out petulantly.

'OK, thanks, we'll try the Bell and Crown then,' I say needlessly over my shoulder.

We walk briskly through the bar, telling the others it's time to go.

Later, inside the ground, the drinking continues. My mate Noel shoves his hands down his pants and pulls out two miniature bottles of brandy which he had stashed next to his genitals so as to get past the stewards on the turnstile.

'Here you go,' he says, twisting the cap from one and tipping a few glugs into my beer. I say 'thanks' in a semi-disgusted sort of a way. Things are getting more boisterous. People all around are singing and throwing beer over each other's heads. A stranger lobs a plastic pint glass across the concourse. It clips me on the shoulder and splashes lager on to my face. I'm briefly annoyed before I remember that, in the current context, this counts as fun. It's his way of extending a hand of friendship. I cheer and join with his song about hating Frank Lampard. He seems happy. At least he's helped wake me up a bit.

Up in the stands I doze off again. Midway through the first half I wake up and hear laughter ringing in my ears. Dozens of fans are pointing and laughing at me. It appears they have also been taking pictures on their mobile phones.

'It's not that boring, mate,' people shout.

'You could have woken me up!' I say to my mates, only to notice that they too have been taking pictures on their mobiles. Noel has texted one to my wife with the word 'mug' written beneath it.

'She won't find that funny at all,' I say to Noel grumpily. 'She'll find that hilarious,' I think to myself bitterly.

We either win the game or lose it. Or possibly draw. It's impossible to tell. My vision has gone blurry, and I've lost track of time, space and reason. The one benefit of this is that the notion of 'tiredness' no longer makes any sense. The combination of fatigue and drunkenness has somehow broken the space–time continuum. I feel like I am now operating in some sort of fourth dimension, where normal rules don't apply. A flurry of episodes unfold in a bizarre, jumbled sequence. There are six of us huddled in the back of a stinking mini-cab. We are pulling up at some services off the M4.

'Where are we? What are we doing here?' I am asking.

'We are getting the lovely drugs,' grins Frank from the front seat. 'This man is getting them for us. Then you will feel all right.'

He gestures at the young Asian bloke behind the wheel. There is loud bass thumping out of his speakers. He has sparkly earrings and a hair-do so modern and spiky it's starting to scare me.

'Are you a chef?' I ask him.

'No,' says Frank. 'He's not a chef. He's a driver who knows how to get the lovely drugs.'

A tiny part of my mind is still working well enough to feel anxious about what may happen if they really do get the drugs. I can't be too careful. Once, when we were driving back from the FA Cup Final in 2006 in a big, fancy limo, they dipped cocktail sausages in cocaine and shoved them up a mate's nose while he was sleeping. And took pictures. They like taking pictures of things.

I notice my brother in the corner of the car. Thank God he's here. At least he'll protect me.

'What do you think I should do about the lovely drugs?' I ask him hoping for a bit of fraternal concern or guidance.

He shrugs and says, 'I dunno. Just keep taking them until you start to feel weird. Then go home.'

It doesn't make me feel any better.

A train station. A train. A mass altercation with a ticket inspector. I lock myself in a toilet and try to sleep. But the stench inside makes me want to gag. I stumble back out and fall asleep curled up on a seat. Someone stuffs an empty packet of Maltesers in my mouth and sticks a fag-end on my ear. Back in London they don't let me go home. We get in a taxi and go to another pub. Everyone buys more alcohol. I stumble into the toilet to have a wee. It is full of loud, drunken men talking in shouty, sweary voices. They are like us but perhaps even more so. I don't know why they are all in the toilets. It seems strange. Frank appears beside me at the urinal.

'Why are we here?' I ask him.

'The drugs, the lovely drugs,' he says again.

'But what about the man in the taxi?' I say.

'Forget about him. I'm meeting a friend here who will help us.'

I drunkenly step back from the urinal and knock into a group of the loud, sweary strangers.

'Mind out, mate,' one of them says. He has wide, aggressive, bloodshot eyes. He looks like he's on drugs. Maybe he's Frank's drug friend.

'Are you Frank's drug friend?' I slur.

'You what?' he snarls back at me.

'Have you got the stuff?' I smirk. His friends seem to be encircling me.

Frank steps towards me and grabs my shoulder.

'No, Sam, this isn't my mate,' he says.

'No, that's right, I'm not your fucking mate', says the angry man.

'These aren't the droids you're looking for!' I laugh, pointing at all the men who have surrounded me. It's all starting to feel a bit rum. Frank starts to shout at them aggressively, and I sort of dance in and out of a few people, feeling strangely playful. 'I know how to sort this situation out,' I think to myself. 'I'll just lie on my back and invite everyone to tickle my tummy. That'll lighten the mood.' Someone pushes my face. I push theirs back. The shouting and swearing gets louder, and the gang of toilet buddies suggest we should leave their toilet. They are impolite. We are outnumbered, so we leave, shouting half-hearted insults as we do so. Back at the bar my pals have started to drift away to their homes anyway. Frank is still going on about his friend and the lovely drugs. He vows never to give up on them. I walk out of the pub into the cold night air. A bus pulls up, and I stumble on without saying goodbye.

When I wake up, all I can see are trees. Trees as far as the eyes can see. Their branches cut bleak, creepy figures against the dark winter sky. I blink three times and hope to see something that looks more like home. I don't. I am in a bus garage somewhere quiet and dimly lit and rural-looking. I stand up suddenly, and my right leg, numbed with pins and needles, gives way beneath me. I stumble towards the door and roll down the steps on to the pavement. I feel humiliated. A mother and her young son step over me as they dismount the bus.

'Where are we?' I ask them from the ground. 'What time is it?'

The mother looks scared, grabs her son and hurries away. To all intents and purposes I am now a vagrant.

I climb back to my feet and try to shake some feeling into my leg. I try to find my bearings. It's not good. It all looks like stupid countryside. How far do London buses actually go? This is like a terrible dream. There is no one around apart from the bus driver, who is still sat in his little driving compartment. I approach him, but he quickly presses a button and the doors shut with an unfriendly hiss.

'Shit,' I think to myself. 'I'm that guy. The one covered in dirt and stinking of beer that everyone wants to avoid eye contact with on the bus. How did this happen?'

I start to walk. It's impossible to tell where. I stick to the road. If I keep walking, I will eventually find a road sign or a landmark. Or a welcoming inn that will offer me food and a bed for the night while I attempt to work out what's happened. But the farther I walk, the narrower the road becomes. It grows darker, and the trees start to encroach on me. I panic and decide to cut across the woodland. I think I can hear traffic in the distance. I trip on a root, twist my ankle and tumble to the floor. I think to myself: 'This has not been a good day out. Not in the least.' I feel ready to give up. I begin to doubt that I will ever find my way home again. I contemplate a new life spent here in the woods, surviving on leaves and pine kernels and slowly developing special squirrel-like climbing abilities. Maybe it wouldn't be so bad. Then I throw up in some bracken.

My phone rings. It's my mate Dave.

'Do you fancy a pint?' he asks.

'A pint? A pint? No, there'll be no more pints,' I mumble.

'You sound pissed. Where are you?' he says.

'No idea', I say.

There is a long pause. Eventually Dave says, 'I'm in the car on the way back from the shops. Stay where you are, work out your bearings and I'll come and pick you up.'

It's a touching gesture, which I throw back in his face. 'It's best you forgot I ever existed!' I say and put the phone down.

I rub my ankle and climb to my feet. I start to limp back up the road I came down. Eventually a light glimmers in the distance. It's coming towards me and getting larger. It's a taxi, right out here in the middle of nowhere. I didn't even know they had black cabs in the countryside. I tell the driver my address and ask him to take me to whatever train station will help me get there quickest. He shrugs, and I get in.

Five minutes later we are pulling up outside my home, and he is asking me for four pounds fifty. 'But, how?' I ask in amazement.

'You were only at the common at the top of the road,' he says. 'Go home and get some sleep, young man.'

He is easily the kindest person I've encountered all day.

I stumble through the front door and make my way to the living room. A fire is glowing, and my wife is watching telly. I stand dramatically in the doorway, clutching its frame and panting. There is dirt on my face and trousers. I probably smell.

'You're still awake,' I say.

'Of course I'm still awake,' she says casually. 'It's only eight o'clock. Did you have a nice time?'

'I had a . . . a . . .' I begin, but it all gets too much. I slump on to the sofa and embrace her. For a moment I feel like I'm going to sob. The cold air and fear have snapped me back to sobriety. The day's varied indignities are rattling through my brain like a slide show. I have not behaved in an adult manner. I have been a dick.

'I'm sorry,' I blurt, my face pressed to her shoulder.

'What for?' she asks.

'For everything. For being a rubbish dad and a rubbish husband.'

'You're not rubbish,' she says.

'I am,' I say, breaking into a remorseful, incoherent monologue. 'All the beer . . . the wankers . . . lovely drugs . . . he was just a chef . . . ticket inspector . . . I thought Frank knew them . . . special squirrel-climbing abilities . . . and it only cost me four pound fifty. Anyway, sorry. I'm useless.'

'Slow down,' my wife says, clutching my face. 'You've been out with your mates. You've got a bit drunk. You've all acted like idiots for a few hours. That was the plan, wasn't it?'

I think about this for a moment.

'S'pose so,' I say meekly.

'Did you take any drugs?'

'No.'

'Did you hurt anyone or get nicked or have a fit?'

'No.'

'You didn't snog some girl or anything, did you?'

'No.'

'Well then, what's the problem?' she concludes. 'The curry delivery man will be here in a minute. *Strictly Come Dancing*'s about to start. Shut up and sit down.'

I fall asleep and, this time, don't wake up for eleven hours.

20
Rocky IV

'. . . So Chimpy McGhee told all the other animals that they could now live in the forest without fear of disease, famine or short-sighted planning permissions issued by the local council.' The baby sits in my arms slowly drifting towards sleep. 'And all the other animals cheered Chimpy's name and thanked him for his bravery. The end.'

As I finish my story, she stretches her arms out across my chest in what I choose to interpret as a cuddle. I nuzzle the top of her head and inhale the comforting whiff of Johnson's Baby Shampoo.

'It's time for bed,' I whisper. She wriggles up closer as I carry her through to her bedroom. I place her softly in her cot and begin to bury her in three cuddly monkeys, two bunnies, a tortoise, a penguin, Iggle Piggle out of *In The Night Garden* and a soft toy of indeterminate species which I reckon is probably a mouse but my wife insists is a really skinny pig. The baby shuts her eyes and smiles. I lean down and kiss her lightly on the forehead.

'Daddy loves you,' I say.

'Erurkh,' she croaks with her eyes shut tight, as if to say, 'Shut up and get out, you soppy tart.'

If tonight is like any of the last fifteen or sixteen nights, she won't be bothering us again for another twelve hours. We'll have time for a nice dinner, a film and perhaps even some hanky-panky. Yep, parenthood is an absolute piece of piss. And it's pretty much all down to my excellent storytelling abilities.

We're approaching Christmas: the business end of the year. I used to sneer at Yuletide merriment. Now, immersed in some sort of Jimmy Stewart fantasy, I am about the most Christmassy bastard you could ever hope to meet. For weeks now I've been telling my little girl Christmas-themed bedtime stories so rich in compelling narrative and heart-warming sentiment that they can only be described as magical. All off the top of my head too. I could be as rich as J. K. Rowling if I remembered to jot any of it down. The details are probably wasted on the baby. She just stares through me vacantly, totally oblivious to the gripping plot lines and life-affirming character arcs. But I think she somehow imbibes the general sentiment. There is a comforting rhythm to the way I speak, which she absorbs through osmosis. It sends her into an almost hypnotic state of sleepy contentment.

I prove this to myself by sometimes reading her chapters from whatever book I happen to have lying next to the bed at the time. The other night I read her six pages from the autobiography of Guildford Four member Gerry Conlon. By applying the same gentle vocal stylings to his tales of police torture and judicial miscarriage as I would to one of Chimpy McGhee's tales of forestry adventure, I had her completely captivated. I pulled off the same trick while reading her an extract from Simon Napier-Bell's *I'm Coming to Take You to Lunch – A Tale of Boys, Booze and*

How Wham! Were Sold to China. It may have been an at times startling account of the gay music impresario's hedonistic romp through 1980s' pop Babylon, but to the baby's ears it was as compelling as any stupid Beatrix Potter classic.

The point is, I get to lie on my bed reading my own book for half an hour every evening and dress it up as an act of studious childcare. Everyone's happy, and absolutely no one gets hurt. Successful fatherhood, I am discovering, is based on a simple system of compromises, deceptions and confidence tricks such as this.

This is just one of the discoveries I have made since my unfortunate day out at the football. I lost it for a moment back then. I mean, all I'd really done was gone out, had a few beers and fallen asleep on a bus. Nothing unusual or particularly regrettable about that, I don't suppose. But it was my reaction to it that was the big problem: I let it get to me. I found myself on the verge of tears, contemplating life as a squirrel. It wasn't pretty, was it? In retrospect, I perhaps judged myself a bit too harshly. I've been doing that a lot lately. Ordinary day-to-day acts of stupidity that would have gone without mention in the past have suddenly taken on vast significance in my mind. Setting fire to the bed, starting a fight in a pub toilet, getting lost in some woods: that sort of stuff comes as naturally as breathing or eating or going to the toilet to an imbecile like me. I've been doing things like that all my life. No point sweating these things: for every stupid thing I do there's usually an act of mild cleverness to balance it out. For instance, I am pretty decent at reverse parking. Focusing on stuff like that usually helps whenever I've felt my self-esteem dip below standard levels. I am an old hand at letting myself down. I know how to handle it. But letting my daughter down is a different matter. What has she done to deserve me?

Now I'm learning not to worry so much. I'll probably always be an idiot on the inside. As long as I act like a decent and responsible adult on the outside, that's all that matters. And that's what I've been doing lately.

And the baby is doing OK. In fact, she seems pretty happy to me. My missus tells me she is generally happy with my all-round fatherly performance too.

'How happy, out of ten, with ten being Teen Wolf's Dad and one being Fred West?' I ask her.

'I'm not getting into that sort of discussion,' she insists.

But I can tell by her eyes that she is giving me a seven and a half – which I am categorising as Jim Robinson from *Neighbours*.

Not bad, but I could do better. I have resolved that staying in watching *The Sopranos* all the time is not necessarily the way forward. It makes me sad, dull and depressed. It was that sort of indolent lifestyle that briefly made me forget how to earn a living, speak to strangers or do up the buttons on a shirt. Equally, acting like a drunken adolescent is unlikely to engender respect from my wife and daughter or make me much happier in the long run either. This is why I am searching for a middle way. Now, Buddhists will tell you that the 'middle way' is the practice of non-extremism, a path of moderation away from the extremes of self-indulgence or self-mortification. For me that means making sure I get home from work in time to do bath-time and trying not to get battered on a school night too often. Make a up a few bedtime stories, get a bit of exercise in, remember to wash my hands after pissing. Grown-up stuff. As long as I tick these boxes, I can feel good about myself as a bloke and as a father. For now anyway: who knows what progress I may make in the future? This time next year I may be an eight and a half (John Peel) or even a nine (God, the father of Jesus).

I know what you're thinking – how come The Almighty comes just below Teen Wolf's dad in the league table of fathers? Well, they're similar characters. They're both single parents, they both possess special powers and they're both entirely fictional. But God loses points for not intervening with a lightning bolt when the Romans crucified his son. The Resurrection was too little too late.

I hope that I will eventually be able to achieve Buddhist-like levels of enlightenment and spiritual balance. Mind you, it'll probably take a bit more research. So far, all I've done is quickly scan Buddhism's Wikipedia entry and find something about striving to awaken the true inner self. I'm not sure I'm ready for that. Disappointingly, there's no mention of how one goes about learning to levitate or break metal bars over your head like those Buddhist monks do. I interviewed one of them once when they came over to do a show at Hammersmith Apollo. He told me about this special 'vibrating hand technique', where you hold your hand an inch from an adversary's forehead and use it to communicate spiritual energy into him through vibrations. It's like a sort of curse. After you've done it, you can kill him any time you want, using brainwaves. You can do it right there and then or leave it for another five years and strike him down when he's least expecting it. I liked this idea a great deal, although I wasn't quite sure how it fitted in with the whole Buddhist ethos of peace and harmony. Mind you, I was conducting the interview through a dodgy translator, who may have skipped some of the pertinent details. Plus, I'm not altogether sure I didn't dream the whole thing.

My point is that if I can manage to be a little bit more like Buddha and a little less of a dick, then I will be a much happier person. Which will probably make my daughter a much happier person too. I'm not sure if it'll make my wife a much happier person, mind you: she seems to prefer it when I am halfway between happy and sad. When I'm proper sad, I mope and moan. But when I'm happy, I mean really happy, I tend to shout and swagger a bit too much. My self-confidence can sometimes sky-rocket, and I'll wake her up in the night with stupid ideas for a film about a talking hat or my designs for a new type of automatic tennis racket. It drives her round the bend. When I finish writing this book, I'll probably send her mental with my own sense of relief and self-congratulation. She's probably planning a holiday with her mum already. I don't blame her.

Anyway, like I say, physical exercise is forming a central plank of my new design for life. And here I am, on a cold winter's morning, running alongside the riverbank with a thin layer of frost forming atop my woolly West Ham hat. I feel brave to be out here this early in the morning. Heroic even. Globules of sweat form on my temples, then squirm into the corners of my eyes. Steam blows from my mouth. John Cafferty's theme to *Rocky IV* pumps into my ears through my headphones.

I thunder past the ducks, the trees and the rowers.

I focus on my breathing: it's smooth, controlled and steady. Not those spluttering, chitty-chitty-bang-bang gasps I used to do whenever I exercised in the old days.

I skip over a dog turd and flob clumsily into the river as John Cafferty sings about the moment of truth drawing near.

My own destination, or moment of truth as Cafferty puts it, is the railway bridge beside my house, where I like to finish my run. I feel like Rocky training for his showdown with Ivan Drago in the wilds of Communist Russia. I don't need Drago's state-of-the-art exercise machines and computerised fitness monitors. All I need is an open track, some running shoes and a bucketload of guts. And a small bottle of Evian, in case I begin to feel dehydrated. This is the only way for a man to train. While Rocky was pursued constantly by KGB agents in old-fashioned Mercedes saloons (a crappy choice of vehicle for an off-road pursuit really – no wonder Communism fell), I am pursued for a 100-metre stretch by two exuberant border terriers, one of which jumps up and tries to bite my penis before I shoo him away and begin to climb the steps of the bridge. When I reach the top, I gaze out across the majestic, winding Thames and the rows of houses and trees that constitute my neighbourhood and try to think of something celebratory and poignant to shout. A bit like when Rocky climbed to the top of that mountain and jeered in defiance at the whole Soviet Union. But I am too exhausted to think of anything decent, so I just shout 'Adrian!' because it seems like a funny thing to do. I notice two teenagers cycling past on their way home from a big night out. One of them flicks me the 'V's. I stretch down, then wander home.

I shower, I shave, I give the baby her milk and put her down for her mid-morning nap.

Then I receive a strange voice mail message on my mobile phone.

'I'm a friend of your grandmother's,' it says. 'She has something for you. Please call immediately.'

Usually, my gran calls me herself and spends twenty minutes shouting 'I can't bloody hear you' down the phone until I just have to hang up (after which I'm certain she continues to shout the same phrase for a further twenty minutes before dropping the receiver and falling into a deep sleep). Nowadays she lives in a home and has a phone-bitch who, when I call back, tells me to visit on Saturday to collect my long-overdue birthday present. I know, I know; it shouldn't take the promise of a gift to make me want to visit my own gran. But what can I tell you? It does.

On Saturday I forgo my trip to the football to take the baby on a day trip to see her great-grandmother at the old people's home (my nan calls it 'the coffin-dodgers'). Day trips with the baby are just one of the things I am doing more of, to make myself feel like a proper, functioning, reliable adult. I fasten her up in her car seat and hit the M4. This is a journey I have done a hundred times before, at high speeds, listening to loud music while simultaneously texting people from my mobile and steering with my knees. But today I drive like a dad. My hands are on the wheel in the ten-to-two position. I stick to the slow lane, driving so cautiously that even old women in Ford Fiestas occasionally ride right up to my bumper and flash their lights. And I sing nursery rhymes all the way. The baby just eyes me with a look of befuddlement from the back seat and occasionally cries.

I arrive at the home and stride excitedly into my gran's room in eager anticipation of what, if past experience has taught me anything, is likely to be at least twenty quid's worth of W.H. Smith's vouchers. She is sat in the corner, looking grumpy and not very pleased to see me.

'Happy Birthday,' she says in her croaky Liverpudlian squawk. Then she throws me this knot of tangled wool and a crumpled sheet of knitting instructions.

'It's a hat for the baby,' she explains. 'You'll have to finish it yourself, I'm too tired.'

Now, I've had some crap presents in my time. Once, when I was ten, my brother gave me a Mars bar which he'd pre-soaked in four-star petrol. But even that didn't compare to this unfinished hat, meant not for me but my child. There's not even a card. She could at least have wrapped it.

'Is this some sort of fucking joke?' I ask.

'I can't bloody hear you,' she replies.

It is immediately apparent that she has only summoned me here to show how annoyed with me she is. She gets like this when I haven't visited her for a while. It's supposed to be a form of corrective punishment. The irony is, it only makes me less likely ever to visit again. What she doesn't realise is that I have a trump card up my sleeve in the form of the baby, whom I have kept hidden beneath a blanket in her pushchair.

'Look who I've brought!' I announce, lifting the blanket with a theatrical flourish to reveal my sleeping offspring.

Gran's head turns slowly like a tortoise. She peers over her spectacles at this tiny, cherubic child. It's a sight of peaceful beauty that could surely melt even the coldest of hearts and combat the most curmudgeonly of moods.

'Fat hands,' says Gran.

'Pardon?' I say.

'The baby. It's got fat hands,' she enunciates in staccato as though I'm the deaf one.

I look down at my daughter's admittedly chubby, almost entirely wristless, hands.

'Yes, I suppose they are a bit fat,' I say.

I suspect this wasn't the sort of response she was looking for. So she tries again.

'And fat legs too. What do you feed her?'

'Lard mainly', I smile, squeezing the baby's voluminous thighs and realising they feel like one of those executive stress gizmos you keep on your desk. 'You look lovely, by the way,' I tell Gran. She turns her face to the window, rolls her eyes and tuts.

The baby wakes up and cries.

'Probably wants her nappy changing,' says Gran. 'I'm not doing it.'

In her mind it probably only seems like last week that I was born. That's probably why she seems so shocked that I am trying to change the baby's nappy myself.

'Bloody hell! What are you doing?' she says, her eyes bulging out of her skull.

'I'm changing its nappy,' I smile, laying the baby on its mat and grabbing the wet wipes from the bag.

'Well, ehm, d'you want me . . .' she is stuttering and muttering in panic. She can't believe her eyes. She thinks the Alzheimer's has taken hold once and for all. 'Do you want me to call a nurse? They'll have the equipment,' she says.

'Don't worry,' I say. 'I do this all the time. I've got all the stuff I need here in the bag,' I say.

'You do it all the time?' says Gran. 'What, really?'

'Yeah. Wait a minute. You do realise that this is my baby, right?'

'Of course I do,' she says, narrowing her eyes and glaring at us both suspiciously. She watches me change the nappy for a while, seemingly deep in thought.

'Your grandfather never changed a nappy in his life,' she eventually says. 'Too lazy.'

'Well, it was different back then, wasn't it?' I say. 'We're more resourceful these days.'

'Oh, listen to him. "Resourceful", is he?' she says, presumably to an imaginary friend in her head. I can detect a tiny glint of respect somewhere in her ordinarily disdainful eyes. I have momentarily impressed her, and she feels slightly ashamed by it.

'Probably quite difficult to change a nappy on a baby that fat,' she says, just to balance things out a bit.

'Yeah, that's right,' I say. 'Impressive, isn't it?'

'They're bringing my lunch in a minute,' she says. 'You'd better go.'

So I leave – feeling just a little more concerned about her than usual. It's not like her to give up so easily on pissing me off. She really is getting on.

Later that evening I am sat with my wife in front of *Nigella Express* eating tea. We are having baked potato with beans and cheese. Nigella is proposing to make a three-course 'supper' for guests in less than half an hour.

'I'm about to beat a 240 millilitre tub of cream with a teaspoon of vanilla!' she beams at us. I haven't got a fucking clue what she's on about. But I know I like it.

'Why can't I be more like Nigella?' I find myself thinking. Then I spill a forkload of baked beans down myself, some of which manage to crawl into the crevices between the cushions of our sofa.

'This is ridiculous!' I unexpectedly announce to my wife. 'We're supposed to be a family, and we should eat like a family! From now on, we'll eat every meal at the dining table!'

She's taken aback by my assertiveness. In my mind she finds it sexually attractive. She certainly seems to be winking at me, but that may just be because I spat a small amount of baked potato in her eye.

The dining table has been playing on my mind for a while now. It seems to symbolise the sort of traditional, almost Victorian, family environment I'd like my daughter to grow up in.

When I was growing up, all we used the dining table for was playing Subbuteo on. Also, our dog Bella used to sleep under there. She was usually good-natured, but she found that fact that we liked to stage table football tournaments on the roof of her home irritating. As an act of revenge she would seize on any Subbuteo equipment we foolishly left out overnight and eat it. She gnawed her way through floodlights, corner flags and, on one disastrous occasion, even players. Midway through our 1987/8 season Bella consumed a whole Atletico Bilbao starting eleven, plus substitutes. It was a massacre that derailed the league season. We wouldn't have minded, but we used Atletico Bilbao to double as Sunderland and even sometimes – at a stretch – Man U.

I want a dining table to mean more to my little girl than flick-to-kick football. I want it to give her a warm sense of belonging and security every time she sits down at it. I want her to exchange witty remarks, intelligent insights and TV viewing suggestions across our table while she eats balanced, heart-healthy meals on a nightly basis.

That's why I have put my foot down. That's also why I have spent a whole hour clearing all the unopened mail and newspapers off it this evening. So we can sit down together and eat. And talk. And experience the sort of moment that bonds a proper family. The table is round and made out of glass. I bought it when I was feeling a bit flush. It's about time we got our money's worth. I sit on one side; my wife sits opposite. The baby is balanced precariously in her high chair between us. We are having omelette with chips and peas followed by Muller Fruit Corners with a glass of Appletiser on the side and no telly or anything.

'So,' I say to my wife, all seriously, 'how was your day?'

'What?' she says with a curl of the lip.

'Your day. How was it?'

'I told you already when I came in. It was shit.' She is back at work.

'Ah yes, of course. Shit, yes.'

'Why are you talking like it was Victorian times?' she asks. It is true that I have affected a posh accent and deep, gravelly burr with which to conduct dining-room conversation. It just seems right.

'Did you happen to read about this business with the economy and what-have-you? Terrible,' I say, ignoring her question about the voice.

'No, I did not,' she says, rolling her eyes at the baby and stabbing a McCain oven chip with her fork.

'No, nor did I,' I say.

There is an awkward silence. We munch our food and stare at the door. The door that leads to the room with the sofas and the telly and the scatter cushions. And then the baby starts to wimper.

'Oh dear, she's crying!' I say. 'Do you think it's this room?'

'Yes, definitely,' says my wife. 'I think she'd be much more comfy next door.'

'Righto, you grab the baby, I'll grab the plates,' I say standing up. 'At least we tried, right?'

'Yep, we tried,' she says, already scuttling off with the infant under her arm.

We're sat down in front of *Hell's Kitchen* just in time to see Jim Davidson booted out. Evenings in don't get much better than this.

21

Spleen

A grim, yellow light flickers from the ceiling. A sickly, surgical smell permeates the room. I stare down at the torn fabric on the seat of my swivel chair and pick idly at the foam inside. My other hand is squeezing my mum's shoulder. Above the monotonous buzz of the light fitting I can hear the voice of the doctor – sad but friendly, encouraging but serious – reading out some medical terms and conditions like they are the small print from the bottom of a dodgy insurance advert.

'There is a reasonably significant risk that your spleen could be ruptured during this procedure,' he deadpans.

My mum nods and smiles nervously. My oldest brother, who is sitting to my left, stares at the wall and looks like he's going to puke. The doctor looks like he's waiting for some sort of response.

'That's shouldn't be a problem,' I say encouragingly. I don't want anyone getting too worried. I think it's best to respond to all of the doc's warnings with a matter-of-fact smile and a shrug. But the fact is, I have no idea what a spleen is. For all I know, it could be the thing that navigates our arms or makes sure our eyes don't pop out of our faces every time we sneeze. Still, I figure you can probably get computerised spleen replacements from Japan now if you're willing to fork out enough dough. Easy for me to act all cavalier, mind you. It's not my spleen he's on about.

My mum keeps nodding and smiling. My brother keeps staring at the wall. The doc goes back to his list.

'There is a significant chance that the colon itself may get damaged, in which case we'll have to fit a colostomy bag,' he says.

My mum looks concerned.

'But that would only be a temporary thing,' I tell her – as though I've got a flaming clue.

'No,' interrupts the doc. 'I'm afraid it would be permanent.'

'Why did he have to go and tell her that?' I think. 'I almost had the poor cow convinced.' Sometimes there's nothing worse than an honest doctor.

I put my arm right round my mum's shoulders and squeeze her tight, as though that might make up in some small way for the fact that she could be shitting into a bag for the rest of her life. She offers me a weak smile of thanks but, for once in her life, is completely lost for words.

'Well, that's about it then,' I say with inappropriate merriment. I half-rise to my feet in a bid to bring an end to the whole unsavoury discussion. I see no point in sitting here listening to the sort of demented, miserable stuff that may or may not happen to my mum when she goes under the knife tomorrow.

But the doc's not finished. He can't finish. He's like a runaway train of bad tidings. He is spewing out worst-case scenarios like he's got bad-news Tourette's. I suppose he's obliged to. If he doesn't outline every last possible eventuality, then one day someone will only lose a spleen and sue the whole NHS on the grounds that they weren't warned about it.

'Hang on a minute! No one ever mentioned anything about losing my spleen! I wouldn't have agreed to the operation had I known!'

'But you'd just been knocked down by a bus. If we hadn't operated, you would have died.'

'That's not the point. That spleen was very dear to me. It was my favourite internal organ. I'm not sure life will be worth living without it. But hand over ten grand of taxpayers' money and we'll call it quits.'

The doctor shifts position, straightens his back and tries to fix my mum's wobbly gaze. I can tell he's gearing up for something major.

'Lastly, I must warn you that there is a risk of death.'

I look at my mum, my mum looks at me, we both look at my brother, my brother looks at the wall. I'm beginning to think he might actually be dead. We look at the doc. The doc doesn't know where to look. What I'm trying to say is, it's awkward.

'They have to say that to everyone,' I tell my mum with what's supposed to be a reassuring wrinkle of the nose.

'No, actually,' says the doc. I can sense that he's starting to find my constant attempts to undermine him slightly irritating. 'This is a major operation. It's likely to last around five hours. Taking into account your age, it poses an above-average risk, I'm afraid.'

My mouth has gone dry, and my head's gone all tingly. My annoyingly upbeat commentary on the whole situation has come to an abrupt halt. I've run out of material. My well of emptily comforting platitudes has run dry. I just sit there and gulp. Now it's my mum putting her arm around me. The doctor breaks the brief silence by smiling warmly and telling my mum with sincerity, 'But we'll do our best to make sure that doesn't happen.'

Then the three of us all have to sign some forms, and the meeting draws to a close. I've been in some rubbish meetings in my time. Budget meetings, marketing meetings, meetings where phrases like 'We'll no longer be needing your services' are used. I've even been in one of those meetings where someone starts throwing an 'ideas ball' around. But however bad those meetings were, at least no one ever informed me that my mother might be about to die. I mean, that really is the mark of a crappy meeting, isn't it? It kind of puts all of the other crappy meetings into context. I'd chuck as many bloody ideas balls around a conference room as I was asked to, as long as no one caught one and said, 'Here's an idea – let's kill Sam's mum.'

But the last half-hour was so much more than just a rubbish meeting. It probably ranks as one of the rubbishest episodes in my entire life. I know she isn't dead yet, but inside my naturally pessimistic mind I am already compiling a funeral playlist and fighting back the tears. Not just at the thought of her death but at the extra misery that will be heaped on if, as would probably be the case, her dying wish was to have songs from the musical *Mamma Mia* played as we enter the chapel of rest.

Yep, this is easily worse than the time I got caught under a lilo at White City swimming baths in 1984. And definitely scarier than the brief moment I thought my wife and child were going to die during the birth all those months ago. That fear came and went in a matter of seconds – it didn't have time to ferment and intensify to this brain-mangling level.

We step out into the waiting room, where other grim-faced patients sit around anticipating similarly bad news, passing the time with two-year-old copies of *Take a Break* magazine. Like that's going to make them feel any better. The gastro-enterology unit is where people go to kiss goodbye to large chunks of their bowels. It's not the jolliest part of the hospital.

The three of us – my brother, my mum and I – shuffle about and mutter. It's weird. We're not usually short of words, my mum and I. My brother hates hospitals, so I half-expected him to go a bit weird. I give him an awkward brotherly hug. He pulls a face that makes him look like he's having a stroke. He's specifically hated this hospital ever since he had to spend three nights here in the late '80s after a jogger smashed his jaw to pieces outside our local boozer. My brother had the drunken audacity to mock his running style and shout the words, 'Go on, my son,' as he ran past, so the jogger turned back and punched him in the face. Then the gutless bastard just ran off in his soppy tracksuit. They rushed my bro to A&E and ended up having to wire up his jaw. He couldn't open his gob more than half an inch for the next six weeks. My mum had to liquidise his meals and serve them to him through a straw. The only minor upside of the whole thing was that he had to grow a beard, which, some people commented, made him look a tiny bit like Jeremy Irons.

No wonder he's looking queasy. My mum, meanwhile, is trying to put a brave face on things.

'I just don't want you boys worrying about me,' she says. This has been her position ever since she broke the news about her cancer a few weeks ago. She was ready to face it; she just didn't want her condition to bother her sons. I could see what she meant. If she died, she'd have nothing left to worry about. We'd be the mugs left sitting around crying our tits off, moaning on about how we miss our mum and boring everyone with tedious, self-indulgent memories of how great she was, like we were living out some sort of Violet Kray fantasy.

Still, this isn't the time to start thinking that sort of thought. This is the time to say inspirational and defiant things like 'You'll get through this!' and 'I know you're strong enough to fight this bastard cancer, goddammit!' But I'm too confused, saddened and tired. I've been here waiting for that stupid, miserable meeting with the doc for the past seven hours. I need some sleep. She needs a bed on the ward, which they say could take another couple of hours to materialise. Other relatives arrive. I hug my mum, tell her I love her, then decide to walk all the way home along the river and have a think. Which is probably the last thing I need.

I should have seen all this coming. Whenever things start to go a bit too well, I get suspicious. I start to think that something rubbish must be lurking for me round the next corner. And I'm quite often right. It's about yin and yang, or whatever you want to call it. The balance of the universe. For every good thing there must be an equal and opposite rubbishy thing. I've got a perfect wife, a gorgeous daughter, a nice home, a decent career, a ginger cat and high-speed wi-fi access in every room. I was approaching content. I was almost happy. I was verging perilously on the edge of smugness. And then my Old Dear calls me at work to say she's got stupid bloody cancer of the colon. Of course she has. It's all so predictable.

I amble along the Thames and try to force my brain to focus on the positives. Like the baby. The way she makes me feel when I see her in the morning. Her little giggles. Her toothy grin. The way she's learned to say 'dada'. Does it help me feel any better? Does it fuck.

Don't get me wrong, that baby is the best thing that ever happened to me. She makes my life seem fulfilling and altogether less pointless than it used to. I miss her every second we're apart. But I can't say her existence has managed to negate the impact of all of life's other irritations. I don't tread in dog shit and think to myself: 'Never mind! Who cares about this new pair of Nike Airs getting ruined when I have been blessed with the wondrous gift of a child?' No, I still think, 'Shit, I'm going to have to go home and scrape that off with a knife.' I hoped fatherhood would give me a broader, more sober perspective on life. It hasn't. If anything, it makes day-to-day problems seem more severe, because I now worry about how they may impact on the baby.

Mind you, she does at least provide a useful distraction from all the other stuff. She is mobile these days. She crawls and climbs and rolls and throws things around. She is able to chuck food at us, pour water over electrical appliances and heave herself across the living-room floor on her arse in the direction of the open fire. This means that I can never relax or take my eye off her for a second. I have had to quickly train my previously flabby and indifferent brain into a focused, attentive and diligent machine. There simply isn't enough time for me to sit around worrying about my mum's cancer or the dog shit on my trainers as much as I'd like to. I am too busy trying to stop her from eating cat food or bursting into flames.

I wake up on the morning of my mum's operation. It's ten to seven. I wonder how I'm going to get through the day without a terrifying mental picture of my mum laid out on an operating table plaguing my every thought. Wondering if the procedure will be successful. Wondering if she's even still *alive*.

My maternal grandma used to tell me, 'Always get out of bed the moment the alarm goes off. No point just lying there. You'll only end up "thinking".' She'd say the word 'thinking' with the sort of disgusted sneer most of us would reserve for the word 'felching'. I always wanted to ask her what her problem was with the notion of thought. Where she thought civilisation might be today if everyone had her sneering attitude towards the use of one's brain. But I never picked her up on it because I was too scared. And now I realise that she may have been right anyway. The world keeps turning, whether you think about it or not, doesn't it? What good does it do to sit around thinking a load of stupid, pointless, egotistical thoughts in the meantime? You'll only get yourself all het up and anxious.

In any case, I've got no choice in the matter these days: when the baby wakes up, I wake up. I stagger into her room, pull open the blinds and approach her cot. She is standing up, clinging on to the bars. She blurts out something that I think is supposed to mean 'hello' and chucks a cuddly penguin at me. I get her up, take her back into our bedroom and dump her on top of my sleeping wife. I go downstairs, make her up a bottle of milk, fix two cups of tea and feed the cat. I get the baby dressed and give her some breakfast. I make myself a bowl of porridge, then see my wife out the door so she can catch the early train to work. I clean the baby's face, which is covered in banana and oats, get her out of her chair and spend fifteen minutes reading her a pop-up book about a renegade farmer with a talking tractor. While I do this, she methodically tears the book to pieces. I make her some pasta with vegetables for her lunch while she sits on the kitchen floor playing with, and occasionally eating, some colourful dough. I pack the pasta into a Tupperware box and stuff it in her change bag along with an apple, a yoghurt, a small tub of raisins, five clean nappies, some wet wipes, some nappy bags, a change of clothes, an emergency bottle of Calpol, a couple of cuddly monkeys and some cream for her arse. I put on her jacket and shoes, put on my jacket and shoes, stick her in her pushchair and wheel her out of the house. Then I walk her to Sophie's house.

With my wife and me back at work, Sophie looks after the baby three days a week. She is brilliant and warm and diligent. She is all the things I should be. She also has an array of toys far more vast, interesting and educational than anything we've got in our house. For this reason, among others, the baby loves going to Sophie's. Very occasionally, she may whimper slightly when I kiss her goodbye. This makes me feel sad. But most days she reaches out to

Sophie with a big smile and ignores me when I kiss her goodbye. This makes me even sadder. Still, I reckon it's better for her to get used to being out and about with other people at an early age. If she hung around the house with me the whole time, she'd just end up like Sloth from *The Goonies*.

I go home. I get changed. I run six miles by the river. I come back, I shower, I shave, I pack my bag for work. And as I make my way towards my nearby office, I realise that it's only ten o' clock and I've already achieved something worthwhile today. I've worked, I've exercised, I've put a smile on my little girl's face. I've helped my wife get off to work and I've tidied the kitchen. I've even steamed some broccoli. I have been a family man. A dad. Not quite Teen Wolf's dad, admittedly. But a dad all the same.

I have less time to get all of my work done because the day is squeezed at either end by childcare responsibilities. There's no time to sit around looking at narcoleptic puppies falling off chairs on YouTube or e-mailing abuse to friends and former colleagues. I have to work with a level of concentration and intensity that is completely unfamiliar to me. I actually quite like it. I get stuff done. I hit deadlines and earn money. It's strangely exhilarating. And best of all, it helps to distract my mind from whatever ghastly predicament my mum is currently in.

In the afternoon I pick up the baby a few hours early and walk her down to the park. It's the first proper sunny day of the year. We walk along the side of the railway tracks with her jabbering inconsequential nonsense at me from the pushchair. I nod and say things like, 'Yes, quite right,' and 'Oh really? Well I never.' It strikes me that this is good conversational practice for when my wife and I are deranged geriatrics with nothing much left to say to each other.

We get to the park and head for the swings and slides. Of course, she's still a bit too young and useless to make proper use of the facilities, but she can sit on my lap while I muck about on the swing, clutching her tightly to my front and listening to her giggle with excitement. It's pretty quiet here. Just three or four people walking dogs in the grassy bit and a smattering of mums pissing about on the see-saws and roundabouts with their kids. I'm the only dad here. I make a big show of having fun with the baby. I encourage her to call me 'dada' as loudly as possible. I'm not trying to show off: in situations like this I just lapse into a form of mental anxiety that I like to call 'nonceanoia'. It's that feeling that dads get when they find themselves in kid-friendly environments like this. You're very often the only bloke around. You feel conspicuous. You feel shifty. You're not so much 'standing around and playing with your child' as 'lurking creepily near other people's children'. Hey, don't blame me for thinking this way – blame *The News of the World*; they're the ones who planted the seeds of paedo-obsessivism in the minds of me and the rest of the nation. I may know that I'm not a nonce, but I'm afraid I can't blame the other mums for giving me suspicious sideways glances. The papers have pumped our minds full of fear. The spectre of predatory paedos hangs over each and every one of us every time we leave the house. For all they know, my baby isn't a real baby at all but a prop fashioned from latex and beads to gain me access to this playground. This is why I'm trying my best to demonstrate loudly the fact that she can speak. 'Who am

I?' I shout gaily at her, loud enough for the other mums to hear. The baby just looks at me blankly, befuddled by my line of questioning.

'Who am I? Am I your dada? That's right! Say "dada"!' Still no response. My insistent tone is making me look even more suspicious and weird. The baby makes an unusual quacking noise that sounds nothing like the word 'dada', then frowns and points urgently at the rocking horse on the other side of the playground. I pick her up and skip over to the horse in a manner that I hope demonstrates my authentic fatherly credentials.

It's one of those long, red horses with six or seven seats along it. I sit the baby on the front one and climb on the seat behind to hold her in place. I'm about to start rocking the contraption when I hear a voice from behind me saying, 'Room for a couple more?' It's a male voice. 'Must be a nonce,' I think to myself casually.

I don't look round. I hear the man's voice conversing with a small boy. I feel them climbing on the seats behind me. I half-turn around and say to the boy, 'Ready?' He nods and I use my feet to start gyrating the horse back and forth. The baby starts to giggle. The boy starts to cheer.

'Do the noise, granddad! Do the noise!' he says. And I hear the man start to make a clippety-clop noise.

I am impressed by the man's horse impersonation. It verges on the uncanny. 'It must be Johnny Morris,' I think. 'But I thought he was dead?' I turn around. It is not Johnny Morris. But I do recognise the face from somewhere. I narrow my eyes and stare at him. He keeps on doing the horsey noise, only slightly more nervously. Then I work it out.

'Mr Martin!' I exclaim.

'Yes,' he says, looking surprised and concerned.

'It's me! Sam! You remember! I was one of your pupils!'

He blinks back at me, trying to register a face he last saw twenty-two years ago, when he was my headmaster at primary school. I beam at him with a strange sense of excited anticipation. I want him to be impressed. I want him to feel proud. Proud that I have grown into a normal, fully limbed human adult with trousers and shoes and coherent words coming out of his mouth. Not some loser degenerate lying in the gutter completely naked but for a thick layer of grime and a dead pigeon strapped around his groin with string, throwing cider everywhere and shouting abuse at him for never giving him the chance to succeed when he was younger. Which, to be fair, is what he might reasonably have expected from me. I want to say, 'Look at me, Mr Martin! Aren't you proud I'm not drunk and mad! Here I am in the park at four in the afternoon, with my daughter, completely sober, being an adult! You helped make this impressive individual you see before you today! How do you feel?'

He eventually says, 'Oh yes, Stuart.'

'No. Sam. My name is Sam.'

'Of course. Sam. I remember.' He eyes me suspiciously. He glances at the baby. He's probably thinking I'm a nonce. Can't blame him for that, I suppose. Still, I'd better clear the matter up.

'This is my daughter!' I say, all pleased with myself. Then I turn to the baby and say, 'This is Mr Martin. He's the big boss man. You must do whatever he tells you!'

I laugh a little too loudly at my own joke. He chuckles awkwardly. I am excited to be exchanging matey yet suitably reverential banter with a man I used to call 'Sir'. It makes me feel grown up, confident and charming. Although I must say he doesn't seem quite up to speed with the whole knockabout nature of the chat. He looks a bit uncomfortable really. Maybe I should stop rocking the horse so vigorously.

'I never thought I'd see the day,' I laugh.

'Hmmm?' he says, not catching my drift.

'That I'd be rocking Mr Martin on a horse. Funny, innit?'

He laughs hesitantly. Perhaps he's beginning to think I'm mad. I suppose I am acting a little bit too over-enthusiastic about what is, after all, a fairly prosaic encounter in the park. Maybe I'm coming across as a bit needy. Maybe I am a bit needy. It's like I've suddenly made a new friend. I must admit I haven't acquired many new mates since I've been living around here. Dave is the only bloke I socialise with locally, but he doesn't count because I'd known him for years. It'd be nice to have a few blokes who I could bump into on my way down the shops and go for a spontaneous pint with. Or someone round the corner with whom I could arrange a Sunday afternoon game of three-and-in down the rec. Ideally, these friends would be of a similar age to me and in possession of hilarious personalities and glamorous yet unintimidating lifestyles. But Mr Martin will do for now.

'Who's this?' I say, looking at the two-year-old lad sat in front of him.

'This is my grandson, James,' he replies.

'Hello, James!' I say, ruffling the boy's hair chummily.

There's still something stiff about his manner. I'm not really sure we're at the stage of having pints or games of three-and-in with each other quite yet. I wonder what I'm doing wrong? Fatherhood seems to have deprived me of what few socialising skills I once possessed.

Mr Martin and James are getting off the horse. As a final throw of the dice I blurt out, 'Remember sports day?'

'Which sports day?' he asks.

'Erm. Any of them?' I say, desperately.

'Well, yes. I remember the sports days.'

'Good, weren't they?' I mumble.

'Yes,' he says with a touch of sympathy creeping into his voice now. 'Yes, they were good.'

There is an awkward silence. He fastens the buttons on James's coat.

'Anyway, nice to see you again, we must be off,' he says.

'Bye then,' I mutter. And then I watch as Mr Martin and James disappear out of the park gates.

The baby looks at me. I can detect a touch of patronising condolence in her eyes. It doesn't feel nice to have been mugged off in front of my own daughter like that. Especially not by my old headmaster. I thought that moment could have been more poetic. It should have verified my passage from youthful tyke to bona fide adult. I don't quite know what I expected from him. Maybe a manly bear hug. Or a short dizzy spell of excitement at the mere sight of my face. Or for him to have instantly confessed: 'I have followed your career closely, Sam Delaney, and I am impressed. I was a particular fan of your fleeting appearance on that documentary about the history of the C word.' Then he might have walked off thinking to himself, 'That one boy vindicates my entire teaching career.'

Who knows why he reacted like he did? Maybe he doesn't read the papers I write for. Maybe he doesn't have access to the obscure digital TV channels I sometimes appear on. Maybe he just gets nervous around former pupils and thinks they're going to head-butt him or something. Personally, I never had much of a problem with the bloke. He was firm but fair really. He also had an impressive way of clicking his fingers while pointing and shouting 'You boy!' during assembly when he spotted me acting the goat. It got to the stage where I acted the goat on purpose just to see his technique in action.

I text my mate Olly in Dubai, saying, 'I just saw Mr Martin.' He texts back immediately, asking, 'Did he do that finger-pointing thing where he clicks his fingers?' I tell him that he didn't. I regret not asking him to do it when I had the chance. I may never see Mr Martin again. And if I do, I get the sense he may avoid me. Olly texts me again.

'Where did you see him?'

'At the swings and slides,' I reply.

'Swing and slides?' Olly texts back. 'What are you? Some sort of nonce?'

I put the baby back in the pushchair and hastily wheel her home.

22
DICKHEAD

Steam hisses from cappuccino machines, and the scent of roasted coffee beans wafts through the air and up my nose. I briefly gag, then sip from my plastic cup of tap water. The baby slurps some babychino from her plastic spoon. My eyes dart across the day's newspaper headlines.

'Global Warming To "Drown Britain" by 2020, Warn Scientists.'

'Terror Threat Set To Intensify, Says Security Chief.'

'Iranian Nuclear Strike "Unavoidable", Claims Diplomat.'

'Mini-Me Beds Chanelle! He Was Like A Jack Russell On Heat, Says Source.'

This is Planet Earth in 2009. The world my daughter will grow up in. A world of environmental catastrophe, terrorism, nuclear war and reality TV stars having it off with dwarfs. A world of 'babychinos'. For the moment I feel safe laughing from the sidelines, assuming I'll be safely dead from natural causes by the time Britain sinks into the North Sea or the Iranians invent a rocket powerful enough to shoot their nukes at whitey. But what of the baby? She'll be reaching maturity just as all of these ugly issues really start to ripen. She'll be on the front line of a world where religious extremists blow up school buses on a daily basis and where one in every two people is a reality TV star willing to have sex not only with dwarfs but with animals and robots and bin bags and slabs of concrete, just to get their picture in the paper. Perhaps the reality TV stars will be having sex with the terrorists. Perhaps there will even be reality TV shows based on becoming a terrorist. *Make Me A Suicide Bomber.* Or even worse, *Bum Me Then Bomb Me!*, in which twelve wannabe Terror WAGs compete to get sodomised then blown up by a Basque separatist. One thing's for sure: the world is spiralling out of control fast. How could I have brought a child into this stinking grotesquery of evil? I am a bad man.

I look at my little angel sitting there, blissfully oblivious of the despicable future she is destined to grow up in, guzzling her babychino like she hasn't a care in the world. The idiot. I mean, there's more air than milk in that tiny cardboard cup. They still charged me a quid for it, mind you. I might just as well have blown in her face for thirty seconds for all the nutrition she's getting from it.

She sticks her nose in the cup, clamps her teeth around the rim, lifts her head up and spills the dregs of watery white liquid down her top. I'm not sure if she's got the wherewithal to survive the apocalypse that is gradually unfurling before her.

I feel a bit guilty and indulgent for not considering all this in the first place. When we decided to have a baby, all we thought about was ourselves. About whether we had enough money, enough space in the house, enough time on our hands and enough love in our hearts. But really, how relevant is that sort of stuff in the long term? The baby is only a baby for a few short months. Before long she'll be a proper human being with her own shit to deal with in the big wide world. By the time she's beginning to face up to the reality of a new life under the sea, I could be dead – having left her with what is likely to be a paltry inheritance and a head load of crappy life advice that will be of even less use to her than it was to me. What do I know about sub-aqua living? I can barely swim.

Shame really, innit?

I rummage through the rest of the paper in search of light relief. Ah, the family section, this ought to lift my spirits. Look, there's a picture of a friendly little tyke with his face painted like a tiger. Sweet.

'Parent Groups Raise Fears Over Toxic Face Paints,' reads the headline.

Bloody hell. Even the family section is intent on souring my mood.

'Salt And Your Baby's Kidneys: The Truth,' shouts another headline on the opposite page.

It gets worse.

'Are You Giving Your Baby Too Much Fluid?'

'How Ethical Are Your Wet Wipes?'

'Who Is Watching The Person Who's Watching Your Child?'

'Macrobiotic Babyfoods: Has The Bubble Burst?'

'How Do You Come To Terms With The Revelation That Your Mother Is A Murderer?'

I involuntarily answer each of the questions inside my head in quick-fire succession.

'Yes! No! Pass! No! I mean yes! I mean, I don't know. Just leave me alone!'

They give you a lot to think about in these newspapers, don't they? No wonder I usually stick to the sport. Some wanker in a rugby shirt nicked that section before I got here. I suppose I could have bought my own paper instead of relying on the coffee shop's complimentary copy, but, at a pound a babychino, I feel morally obliged to make the most of all of the facilities this place has to offer.

The family section is even more disconcerting than the proper news bit. At least I can pretend all that stuff that's going on in the Middle East or the North Pole or wherever doesn't really exist. None of it really affects me directly. I can just skim those stories, stroke my chin, look a little bit concerned and try to crib enough pertinent facts to look knowledgeable if it ever comes up in conversation with friends. Which it probably won't, seeing as I specifically seek out complacent and idiotic friends in order to avoid those sorts of conversation.

But this parental stuff is worrying. Or rather, it suggests there is stuff worth worrying about that I haven't ever bothered to worry about. Which is, in itself, quite worrying, if you see what I mean. Perhaps I should read the stories and make my own mind up? No, that would be ridiculous. There's no time. And I have no interest. My advice? If the baby's crying, give it a Milky Bar.

I look around the coffee shop on this fine Saturday morning. It's jam-packed with happy-looking, well-heeled families feeding their kids expensive milky foam and eating pastries. They haven't got a bleeding care in the world. Good luck to them. They are living in a Utopia where food and sanitation are plentiful and the worst real anxiety you ever experience is suddenly realising on the way into work that you forgot to leave any food out for the cat. We are living in a pampered, Western, conflict-free Nirvana. We have literally run out of things to worry about. But this has left a gaping void in the part of the human brain reserved for fear. It needs to be filled with something. So we invent stuff to shit ourselves about. (I sound like Michael Moore or Noam Chomsky or David Icke, don't I? But there is a crucial difference. Whereas they say these sorts of things because they are passionate believers in them, I say these sorts of things because I'm looking to justify my own lazy ignorance.)

It's probably the same deal with the real news too. None of it's as bad as it seems. I mean, my parents had to raise kids under the very real spectre of the Cold War and the possibility of full-blown nuclear Armageddon. It wasn't a case of 'Iran *may* have a bomb that they *may* one day work out how to let off'. It was more a case of 'Russia *really* have got *loads* of bombs that they are *really* going to fire at us any moment now'.

And as for the environment, they didn't even know about the environment back in the '70s. The word hadn't been invented yet. They were all breezing about doing mad anti-environmental stuff without even realising it was wrong. They'd have Tupperware parties where they all burned the Tupperware and giggled as they watched the poisonous fumes drift into the earth's atmosphere and slowly murder the ozone layer. They would get drunk and spray aerosols at the sun for kicks. Americans would blow up petrol stations on the 4th of July using government funding just to see the pretty colours. Millionaires would pay through the nose to chase polar bears around glaciers in four-wheel-drive gas-guzzlers, firing bullets at them made out of elephant tusks and dangerous chemicals. They were wantonly destroying the planet, and no one was even telling them to stop it.

These days we're still wantonly destroying the planet, but at least there are loads of people making us feel guilty about it. This guilt has even managed to get idiots like me separating their plastics from their glass in the recycling bins. And while it's likely that small acts like this won't make a blind bit of difference in the scheme of things, it's all a step in the right direction. By the time my daughter is grown up, the entire population of the world will be on board. Her generation will be raised to feel guilty about the environment every single second of every single day of their lives. Recycling stuff and remembering to switch off the TV at night will be second nature to them. Saving the planet will no longer be seen as the preserve of stinking hippies and peace freaks but of perfectly ordinary slobs like us. As a result, the planet will probably be saved by the time my daughter is eighteen. Long before Britain gets anywhere near sinking into the sea anyway.

I fold up the paper and put it back on the communal paper rack. Ah, that's better. I have been wholly convinced by my own garbled line of reasoning. Everything is right in the world, and no one has got anything to worry about – all thanks to my brilliant brain. The baby seems to sense this fact and screams with excitement, then tips what's left of my water over my lap. It looks like I've pissed myself. I don't care, not with the future looking this rosy.

The door opens, and in walks Dave pushing his little girl in a buggy. They come over. My daughter and his daughter eye each other suspiciously.

'You look like you've pissed yourself,' remarks Dave.

This is where Dave and I now meet on weekend afternoons. Not the pub. Not the rec for a game of three-and-in. Not even round one of our houses for a session on the Xbox. Here in a coffee shop, like a couple of big girls.

'What are you drinking?' I say, rising to my feet.

'I dunno, what are you drinking?' asks Dave.

'Tap water.'

'But it's a coffee shop,' he says nervously. 'Shouldn't we have a coffee?'

'Hey! They can't tell us what to drink! I hate coffee, and I've given up pretending otherwise.'

'You're right!' he says, visibly inspired by my rhetoric. 'I hate coffee too! It tastes like poison and makes me feel ill. Fuck them. Get me a tap water.'

'Anything for the littlun?'

'She'll have a babychino.'

That's what Dave and I are like these days. We are assertive. We will not just roll over and drink whichever hot beverages 'The Man' says we should drink. We drink our own beverages on our own terms. And sometimes they may not even be hot. Why? Because we're men, that's why. More than that: we are dads. We have grown into our roles. We have learned that you don't become that sort of bloke overnight. You can't force it. You can't make yourself become more decisive or sensible. You don't automatically start choosing to meet up at the coffee shop rather than the boozer. But it happens gradually, because time teaches you that doing these things just makes life easier. We don't even feel like we're sacrificing anything by being here sipping water instead of in the pub guzzling sambuca and gin. We choose to be here of our own free will. It just seems simpler and more pleasant not to be drunk in charge of the babies. It sounds weird, I know, but there it is.

We even look better. Fresher, more rested, less confused and red in the face. We have slowly harnessed our new lives as semi-responsible adults. Dave's eye no longer twitches. I am a bit balder than I was a year ago, but even that's not so bad: it makes me feel more daddish.

'We're having a second,' says Dave.

'A second what?' I ask.

'A second kid.'

'Brilliant,' I say. Actually, it comes out more like '*Brilliant?*' just to be on the safe side.

'Yeah,' he nods earnestly. 'It is brilliant.'

He pauses and pretends to be thinking serious thoughts.

'Becoming a dad is . . .'

'A journey?' I interrupt.

'Yeah. How did you know I was going to say that?'

'Because that's what you told me about eighteen months ago. About two months before you told me that becoming a dad ruins your life.'

'Yeah, well, I've gone back to thinking of it as a journey now.'

'What sort of a journey?'

'Well, it's got its ups and downs,' he says. 'There are moments where you think it's ruined your life. And other moments where you think it's the best thing ever.

And mostly moments where you think it's all right really and not half as much of a hassle as you thought it'd be.'

'I agree,' I say – because I do. 'So what made you decide to have a second?'

'Well, the missus wants to, and my attitude is "In for a penny, in for a pound". Know what I mean?'

'Fair dos,' I say. Then we drain our waters and stroll out of the coffee shop.

I've bought a chocolate brownie to share with the baby when we get home. I decide to text my mum to tell her about this. My mum is obsessed like a demented addict with baked goods of all forms. I use it as a way of tormenting her.

'I've got a chocolate brownie to have with my tea,' I write.

Just as I'm approaching my front door, my phone beeps with her response.

'Well, I'm round my cousin's house having a slice of date and walnut cake,' it reads. 'So up yours, you cunt! Xxx'

Suffice to say, my mum is better. The doctor managed to cut the cancerous growth out of her intestines without rupturing her spleen, damaging her bowels or killing her. He did a nice clean job of it, and she was out of the hozzy after four days. She didn't even have to have chemo or anything. In fact, it all culminated in such an implausibly happy outcome that, if it were the plot to a thriller, you'd be half-expecting a last-minute twist in which her spleen suddenly bursts out of her stomach at a family gathering and bounces round the room infecting the rest of us with a fatal form of cancer. Or something. But nothing like that happened. And I have put a ban on my brain thinking those sort of paranoid, pessimistic thoughts from now on.

I feel like I've learned to cherish the good times. When mum was ill, all I did was yearn for those moments when there was nothing serious to worry about. From now on I've resolved not to sully those carefree moments by inventing stupid, imaginary worries. Not just for my sake but for my daughter's too. She doesn't want to grow up with a father who's riddled with self-doubt and worry. Dads shouldn't spend their time fretting. They should accept themselves and get on with it. They should be pillars of certainty and calm. From this point forward that's the sort of man I'm going to be. Or at least, that's how I'm going to act.

Anyway, you can tell my mum's better by the way she's swearing and eating cake again. These are her two favourite pastimes. The idea of her cramming slices of home-baked date and walnut into her gob while calling me a cunt via text message reminds me how lucky I am to have her around.

That evening she has a party to celebrate the fact she didn't die. It's in a room above a boozer in Hammersmith. The evening sun shines brightly through the windows as friends and family start to gather. There's sandwiches, chicken legs, the lot. There's even a few quid behind the bar. My mum's insisted on playing songs from *Mamma Mia* on the pub stereo, but I suppose you can't have everything.

My older sister is there. That's right, the one they had adopted all those years ago. She ended up getting in touch about a year after my mum told me about her existence.

Her name's not Caroline any more; it's Annie. She's married with two kids of her own, and they're all part of the family. That was another thing that turned out suspiciously well. I assumed she'd turn out to be a drug addict or a thief or a killer or, I dunno, a racist or something. But no, she's lovely. You couldn't hope for a better big sister. Interestingly, despite having not grown up with us or been subject to the same cultural influences, she is very similar in personality to my brothers and me. Only, you know, kinder, smarter and less of a dick.

'Come on, everyone, let's have a toast! Mum hasn't got arse cancer any more!' shouts one of my brothers just as Abba's 'Gimme Gimme Gimme (A Man After Midnight)' has drawn to a close on the stereo. Everyone looks round at him, drunkenly swaying about with his plastic glass of champagne held aloft. See what I mean? Dick.

Mind you, he's a lovable dick. Which, when it comes down to it, is the best you can hope for in a relative. At least, it's the best I can hope for. A good honest bunch of lovable dicks: that's what all the people who surround me tonight are. I look around at them all: half-cut and swaying, talking bollocks, eating cake and generally feeling happy about Mum not being dead. I'm lucky to have them, I suppose. I think about the baby at home being looked after by a friend. And I hope that one day she'll grow up to think of me as a lovable dick. Maybe just lovable and not a dick at all. But either way is fine really. I hug my wife – about the only non-dick I know. And I say a little thanks in her ear for not minding that I can be such a dick sometimes. I don't think she hears me properly because she responds by saying, 'Quarter to nine, I think.' I kiss her and contemplate a future of more little babies, all of whom will hopefully see me as a lovable dick.

The next day I'm having lunch with my wife and daughter. I say lunch: it's only midday. But the days start earlier when you're a dad. You have elevenses at nine, lunch at twelve, dinner at six and sometimes even have breakfast before you go to bed at night. I am a bit hungover in a silly, slightly euphoric way. We are in one of those restaurants we avoided like the plague before we had a kid: it's packed with screaming children, the menu is made up entirely of things you can dip in ketchup and the tablecloths double as painting canvases.

A little girl of about three is giving her dad grief on the next table.

'I don't want this,' she grumbles, regarding her bowl of pasta with a disgusted sneer.

'But it's what you ordered, darling,' he says kindly.

'It looks funny.'

'It's just how you have it at home,' he pleads.

'No it's not. I want something else. I want chips,' she insists.

The dad looks at his wife. The wife shrugs in resignation. He calls the waiter over and orders a bowl of chips.

'That's what we've got ahead of us,' I tell my wife.

'Not if we nip that kind of thing in the bud early,' she says.

'Quite right,' I say, gazing sternly at our daughter, who is looking worryingly toddler-like these days. 'If this one gives me any of that crap, I won't stand for it.'

'Exactly,' my wife agrees. 'It's just a matter of telling her she eats what she's given or nothing at all.'

'Yeah!' I say, warming to the theme. 'You've got to lay it on the line. I'll tell her straight: "I am prepared to let you starve to death if necessary."'

My wife narrows her eyes in thought.

'I'm not sure that's the right way to put it,' she says.

'Of course it is!' I say. 'You need to show them that their destiny is in their own hands.'

'Is that out of *Spiderman*?' she asks.

'No!' I protest before realising it might be. 'Hang on, maybe. Either that or *Star Wars*. I'm not sure.'

She goes back to examining the menu. I go back to surveying the restaurant. The level of behaviour is nothing short of despicable. Worse than anything I've ever seen in a boozer or at the football. Kids are fighting and puking and weeing. It's like the last days of the Roman empire. The funny thing is, I find it strangely relaxing. These sorts of restaurant are the only places you can take your kid without fear of upsetting or disturbing anyone. Our daughter can cry and shout and lob chips across the room with gay abandon, and no one will bat an eyelid. For once I can sit back and let her wreak havoc from her high chair without giving a flying fuck.

Who knew I'd find so much happiness in a high-street burger chain? That's the thing about fatherhood: you discover a whole new set of ways to be happy. Plus, you get to pretty much keep all your old ways of being happy too. As long as you manage to get the balance right, you can effectively treble your daily fun quota. And by extension, make yourself at least four times happier in real terms. And that's not just my personal opinion: that is mathematical fact. I think you'll find my numbers add up.

Some people may deem this new life a sell-out, but how can I be a sell-out when I am enjoying the company of my family over a plate of microwaved onion rings while simultaneously sporting a pair of box-fresh, rare Nike Air Pegasus 89s? See, I'm getting the best of both worlds! I'm living the dream! In your face, rest of the world!

ACKNOWLEDGEMENTS

Huge thanks to everyone who helped me with this book: my agent Matthew Hamilton, my editor Bernard Dive, Rowan Yapp, who first approached me about the idea, and everyone else at John Murray including Roland Philipps, James Spackman, Shona Abhyankar, Mandi Jones, Polly Ho-Yen, Nikki Barrow, Caroline Westmore and Caroline Lotinga.

Thanks also to Mark Law and everyone at the *First Post* who first gave me a forum in which to harp on about the trivialities of my day-to-day existence.

Special mentions to Kevin Curtis for the film, Ian Prytherch for the needles and Andy Friedlander for the tea and biscuits.

I would also like to express my immense respect for the good people of Hungary, a beautiful land rich in noble culture and history. Since completing this book I have learned much of your proud people and the great contributions they have made to the human race.

Finally, I am massively grateful to everyone who helped Coco and I through our first year together, especially: Bren, Baz, Chris Payne, Peter Pallai, Maddy, Mopsy (you're too nice to possibly be mentioned anywhere else in this book), Coach Pete, Sophie Wright, Joseph, Frankie and Ella.

Biggest thanks of all, as always, to the love of my life, Anna.

Read more . . .

Michael Moran

SOD ABROAD: WHY YOU'D BE MAD TO LEAVE THE COMFORT OF YOUR OWN HOME

Ever written a postcard that says 'Wish we weren't here?'

Going on holiday? You must be mad. OK, it's not *absolutely* certain that you'll catch a fatal bout of food poisoning or be banged up in jail as a drugs mule. But you *might*. Why would a sane person risk it? Holidays aren't economical, they aren't ecological and they're not much bloody fun.

With travel tips, handy warnings and lists of stuff you can only do at home, *Sod Abroad* will help you kick the holiday habit. Instead, why not spend a fortnight on your sofa, in your home, watching your telly and eating food that you can actually pronounce?